GONE WITH THE WIND

Margaret Mitchell

TECHNICAL DIRECTOR Maxwell Krohn
EDITORIAL DIRECTOR Justin Kestler
MANAGING EDITOR Ben Florman

SERIES EDITORS Boomie Aglietti, Justin Kestler
PRODUCTION Christian Lorentzen, Camille Murphy

WRITERS Brian Phillips, Julie Hollar
EDITORS Jesse Hawkes, Emma Chastain

This edition published by Spark Publishing

Spark Publishing
A Division of SparkNotes LLC
120 Fifth Avenue, 8th Floor
New York, NY 10011

02 03 04 05 SN 9 8 7 6 5 4 3 2 1

Please send all comments and questions or report errors to
feedback@sparknotes.com.

Library of Congress information available upon request

Printed and bound in the United States

RRD-C

ISBN 1-58663-516-6

Introduction: Stopping to Buy Sparknotes on a Snowy Evening

Whose words these are you *think* you know.
Your paper's due tomorrow, though;
We're glad to see you stopping here
To get some help before you go.

Lost your course? You'll find it here.
Face tests and essays without fear.
Between the words, good grades at stake:
Get great results throughout the year.

Once school bells caused your heart to quake
As teachers circled each mistake.
Use SparkNotes and no longer weep,
Ace every single test you take.

Yes, books are lovely, dark, and deep,
But only what you grasp you keep,
With hours to go before you sleep,
With hours to go before you sleep.

Contents

CONTEXT

MARGARET MITCHELL WAS BORN in Atlanta, Georgia, in 1900. Her father was a lawyer and the president of the Atlanta Historical Society, and her mother was a suffragette (a woman in support of extending the right to vote, especially to women) and an advocate of women's rights in general. Mitchell grew up listening to stories about Atlanta during the Civil War, stories often told by people who had lived through the war. Mitchell attended Smith College, a women's college in Northampton, Massachusetts. In 1919, she returned to Atlanta and began to live a lifestyle considered wild by the standards of the 1920s. After a disastrous first marriage, Mitchell began a career as a journalist and married an advertising executive named John Robert Marsh. In 1926, encouraged by her husband, Mitchell began to write the novel that would become *Gone with the Wind*. She went through nine complete drafts of the thousand-page work, setting an epic romance against the Civil War background she knew so well. In the first eight drafts, the protagonist was called Prissy Hamilton, not Scarlett O'Hara (as the character was renamed in the final draft).

Gone with the Wind differs from most Civil War novels by glorifying the South and demonizing the North. Other popular novels about the Civil War, such as Stephen Crane's *The Red Badge of Courage*, are told from a Northern perspective and tend to exalt the North's values. Mitchell's novel is unique also for its portrayal of a strong-willed, independent woman, Scarlett O'Hara, who shares many characteristics with Mitchell herself. Mitchell frequently defied convention, divorcing her first husband and pursuing a career in journalism despite the disapproval of society.

Gone with the Wind was published in 1936, ten years after Mitchell began writing it. A smash success upon publication, *Gone with the Wind* became—and remains even now—one of the best-selling novels of all time. It received the 1937 Pulitzer Prize. In the late 1930s a film version of the novel was planned, and David O. Selznick's nationwide search for an actress to play Scarlett O'Hara captivated the nation's attention. The resulting film starred Vivien Leigh and Clark Gable as Scarlett O'Hara and Rhett Butler, and it quickly became one of the most popular motion pictures of all time.

Mitchell was less than thrilled by the sweeping popularity of her work. She found the spotlight uncomfortable and grew exhausted and ill. *Gone with the Wind* is her only novel, though she continued to write nonfiction. Mitchell volunteered extensively during World War II and seemed to regain her strength. In 1949 a car struck and killed Mitchell while she was crossing Peachtree Street in Atlanta.

Many critics question the literary merit and outdated racial stances of *Gone with the Wind*. Some consider the novel fluffy, partly because women of Mitchell's time rarely received credit for serious literary fiction and partly because the novel features a romance along with its historical plot. Both blacks and whites have harshly criticized Mitchell's sympathetic depiction of slavery and the Ku Klux Klan and her racist depiction of blacks. The novel is most valuable if read with an understanding of three historical contexts: our own, Mitchell's, and Scarlett's.

PLOT OVERVIEW

I T IS THE SPRING OF 1861. Scarlett O'Hara, a pretty Southern belle, lives on Tara, a large plantation in Georgia. She
concerns herself only with her numerous suitors and her
desire to marry Ashley Wilkes. One day she hears that Ashley is engaged to Melanie Hamilton, his frail, plain cousin
from Atlanta. At a barbecue at the Wilkes plantation the next day,
Scarlett confesses her feelings to Ashley. He tells her that he does
love her but that he is marrying Melanie because she is similar to
him, whereas he and Scarlett are very different. Scarlett slaps Ashley and he leaves the room. Suddenly Scarlett realizes that she is
not alone. Rhett Butler, a scandalous but dashing adventurer, has
been watching the whole scene, and he compliments Scarlett on
being unladylike.

The Civil War begins. Charles Hamilton, Melanie's timid, dull
brother, proposes to Scarlett. She spitefully agrees to marry him,
hoping to hurt Ashley. Over the course of two months, Scarlett and
Charles marry, Charles joins the army and dies of the measles, and
Scarlett learns that she is pregnant. After Scarlett gives birth to a
son, Wade, she becomes bored and unhappy. She makes a long trip
to Atlanta to stay with Melanie and Melanie's aunt, Pittypat. The
busy city agrees with Scarlett's temperament, and she begins to see a
great deal of Rhett. Rhett infuriates Scarlett with his bluntness and
mockery, but he also encourages her to flout the severely restrictive
social requirements for mourning Southern widows. As the war
progresses, food and clothing run scarce in Atlanta. Scarlett and
Melanie fear for Ashley's safety. After the bloody battle of Gettysburg, Ashley is captured and sent to prison, and the Yankee army
begins bearing down on Atlanta. Scarlett desperately wants to
return home to Tara, but she has promised Ashley she will stay with
the pregnant Melanie, who could give birth at any time.

On the night the Yankees capture Atlanta and set it afire, Melanie
gives birth to her son, Beau. Rhett helps Scarlett and Melanie escape
the Yankees, escorting them through the burning streets of the city,
but he abandons them outside Atlanta so he can join the Confederate Army. Scarlett drives the cart all night and day through a dangerous forest full of deserters and soldiers, at last reaching Tara. She
arrives to find that her mother, Ellen, is dead; her father, Gerald, has

lost his mind; and the Yankee army has looted the plantation, leaving no food or cotton. Scavenging for subsistence, a furious Scarlett vows never to go hungry again.

Scarlett takes charge of rebuilding Tara. She murders a Yankee thief and puts out a fire set by a spiteful Yankee soldier. At last the war ends, word comes that Ashley is free and on his way home, and a stream of returning soldiers begins pouring through Tara. One such soldier, a one-legged homeless Confederate named Will Benteen, stays on and helps Scarlett with the plantation. One day, Will brings terrible news: Jonas Wilkerson, a former employee at Tara and current government official, has raised the taxes on Tara, hoping to drive the O'Haras out so that he might buy the plantation. Distraught, Scarlett hurries to Atlanta to seduce Rhett Butler so that he will give her the three hundred dollars she needs for taxes. Rhett has emerged from the war a fabulously wealthy man, dripping with earnings from his blockade-running operation and from food speculation. However, Rhett is in a Yankee jail and cannot help Scarlett. Scarlett sees her sister's beau, Frank Kennedy, who now owns a general store, and forges a plan. Determined to save Tara, she betrays her sister and marries Frank, pays the taxes on Tara, and devotes herself to making Frank's business more profitable.

After Rhett blackmails his way out of prison, he lends Scarlett enough money to buy a sawmill. To the displeasure of Atlanta society, Scarlett becomes a shrewd businesswoman. Gerald dies, and Scarlett returns to Tara for the funeral. There, she persuades Ashley and Melanie to move to Atlanta and accept a share in her lumber business. Shortly thereafter, Scarlett gives birth to Frank's child, Ella Lorena.

A free black man and his white male companion attack Scarlett on her way home from the sawmill one day. That night, the Ku Klux Klan avenges the attack on Scarlett, and Frank ends up dead. Rhett proposes to Scarlett and she quickly accepts. After a long, luxurious honeymoon in New Orleans, Scarlett and Rhett return to Atlanta, where Scarlett builds a garish mansion and socializes with wealthy Yankees. Scarlett becomes pregnant again and has another child, Bonnie Blue Butler. Rhett dotes on the girl and begins a successful campaign to win back the good graces of the prominent Atlanta citizens in order to keep Bonnie from being an outcast like Scarlett.

Scarlett and Rhett's marriage begins happily, but Rhett becomes increasingly bitter and indifferent toward her. Scarlett's feelings for Ashley have diminished into a warm, sympathetic friendship, but

Ashley's jealous sister, India, finds them in a friendly embrace and spreads the rumor that they are having an affair. To Scarlett's surprise, Melanie takes Scarlett's side and refuses to believe the rumors.

After Bonnie is killed in a horse-riding accident, Rhett nearly loses his mind, and his marriage with Scarlett worsens. Not long after the funeral, Melanie has a miscarriage and falls very ill. Distraught, Scarlett hurries to see her. Melanie makes Scarlett promise to look after Ashley and Beau. Scarlett realizes that she loves and depends on Melanie and that Ashley has been only a fantasy for her. She concludes that she truly loves Rhett. After Melanie dies, Scarlett hurries to tell Rhett of her revelation. Rhett, however, says that he has lost his love for Scarlett, and he leaves her. Grief-stricken and alone, Scarlett makes up her mind to go back to Tara to recover her strength in the comforting arms of her childhood nurse and slave, Mammy, and to think of a way to win Rhett back.

CHARACTER LIST

Scarlett O'Hara The novel's protagonist. Scarlett is a pretty, coquettish Southern belle who grows up on the Georgia plantation of Tara in the years before the Civil War. Selfish, shrewd, and vain, Scarlett inherits the strong will of her father, Gerald, but also desires to please her well-bred, genteel mother, Ellen. When hardships plague Scarlett, she shoulders the troubles of her family and friends. Scarlett's simultaneous desire for the Southern gentleman Ashley and the opportunistic New Southerner Rhett Butler parallels the South's struggle to cling to tradition and still survive in the new era.

Rhett Butler Scarlett's third husband, and a dashing, dangerous adventurer and scoundrel. Expelled from West Point and disowned by his prominent Charleston family, Rhett becomes an opportunistic blockade-runner during the war, emerging as one of the only rich Southern men in Atlanta after the war. Rhett proves himself a loving father and, at times, a caring husband. Though he loves Scarlett, his pride prevents him from showing her his love, and it even leads him to brutality. Candid, humorous, and contemptuous of silly social codes, Rhett exposes hypocrisy wherever he goes. He represents postwar society, a pragmatic, fast-paced world in which the strong thrive and the weak perish.

Ashley Wilkes The handsome, chivalrous, and honorable heir to the Twelve Oaks plantation near Tara. Ashley bewitches Scarlett through most of the novel. After the war, Ashley becomes resigned and sad, and he regrets not marrying Scarlett. Committed to his honor and Southern tradition, he cannot adjust to the postwar South. Ashley represents the values and nostalgia of the Old South.

Melanie Hamilton Wilkes The frail, good-hearted wife of Ashley Wilkes. Melanie provokes Scarlett's jealous hatred throughout most of the novel. After the two women suffer together through the Civil War, however, a strong bond forms between them. Eventually, Scarlett understands that Melanie's unflagging love and support has been a source of strength for her. Like Ashley, Melanie embodies the values of the Old South, but in contrast to Ashley's futile dreaming, Melanie faces the world with quiet but powerful inner strength.

Gerald O'Hara Scarlett's father. Gerald is a passionately loyal Confederate who immigrated to America from Ireland as a young man. His strong will, tendency to drink, and selfishness echo in Scarlett's nature. Scarlett also inherits Gerald's love for the South and for his plantation, Tara.

Ellen O'Hara Scarlett's mother, and a descendent of the aristocratic Robillard family. Ellen marries Gerald and devotes herself to running Tara after her father forbids her love affair with Philippe, her cousin. Refined and compassionate, strong and firm, Ellen serves as an impossible ideal for the willful Scarlett. Even after Ellen's death, Scarlett struggles with the competing desires to please her mother and please herself.

Mammy Scarlett's childhood nurse. Mammy is an old, heavyset slave who was also nurse to Scarlett's mother, Ellen. Loyal and well-versed in Southern etiquette, Mammy keeps Scarlett in line. After Ellen's death, Mammy becomes for Scarlett one of the only living reminders of the Old South.

Frank Kennedy Scarlett's weak-willed but kind second husband. Frank is described as an "old maid in britches." Scarlett steals him away from her sister Suellen so that he will pay the taxes necessary to save Tara.

Charles Hamilton Melanie's brother and Scarlett's first husband. Charles is a timid and bland boy for whom Scarlett feels no love. Charles's death early in the war confines Scarlett to the role of widow. Scarlett finds the social expectations surrounding widowhood—that she wear a black veil, for example, and refrain from laughter and pleasure—overly restrictive.

Aunt Pittypat Hamilton Melanie and Charles Hamilton's aunt. Aunt Pittypat is a flighty old maid who faints from shock several times a day. Scarlett lives with Aunt Pittypat for much of her stay in Atlanta.

Bonnie Blue Butler Scarlett's third and last child. Bonnie is the daughter of Rhett Butler. Spoiled and strong-willed like her mother, Bonnie elicits utter devotion from Rhett and eventually replaces Scarlett as the center of Rhett's attention.

Suellen O'Hara Scarlett's younger sister. Suellen is a selfish, petty girl who marries Will Benteen after Scarlett steals Frank from her.

Carreen O'Hara Scarlett's youngest sister. Carreen is a good-natured girl who turns to religion after the war and joins a convent.

India Wilkes Ashley's cold and jealous sister. India never forgives Scarlett for stealing Stuart Tarleton from her during their youth. At one point India catches Scarlett embracing Ashley and gossips about the sight, causing a great debate among all of Atlanta society.

Big Sam The gigantic slave and foreman of the field hands at Tara. Big Sam saves Scarlett from her attacker in Shantytown.

Pork Gerald O'Hara's first slave. Pork is loyal and devoted to the O'Haras.

Prissy   The daughter of Dilcey, a slave at Twelve Oaks. Prissy is a foolish, lazy young slave prone to telling lies. The late discovery of Prissy's lie that she knows how to assist at childbirth compels Scarlett to deliver Melanie's baby herself, which is one of Scarlett's first significant acts of self-sufficiency.

Emmie Slattery A young woman whose poor white family lives in the swamp bottom near Tara. Emmie is considered "white trash," and Scarlett's class-conscious, genteel society dislikes Emmie, as does the narrator.

Jonas Wilkerson The Yankee overseer of Tara whom Gerald fires for impregnating Emmie Slattery. Jonas works for the Freedmen's Bureau after the war and marries Emmie. He raises taxes on Tara to try to force out the O'Haras, prompting Scarlett's marriage to Frank Kennedy.

Belle Watling An Atlanta prostitute with whom Rhett Butler has a long-term affair. She wins the gratitude of the Atlanta Ku Klux Klan by providing them with an alibi for a murder.

Will Benteen A one-legged Confederate soldier who becomes a fixture at Tara after the war despite his lack of family or wealth. Will makes Tara a marginally profitable farm. His competence allows Scarlett to move to Atlanta and leave him in charge.

Wade Hampton Hamilton Scarlett's oldest child. The son of Charles Hamilton, Wade inherits his father's timid and bland disposition.

Ella Lorena Kennedy Scarlett's second child. Ella Lorena is the ugly, silly daughter of Frank Kennedy.

ANALYSIS OF MAJOR CHARACTERS

SCARLETT O'HARA

The protagonist of *Gone with the Wind*, Scarlett is a dark-haired, green-eyed Georgia belle who struggles through the hardships of the Civil War and Reconstruction. Scarlett exhibits more of her father's hard-headedness than her mother's refined Southern manners. Although initially she tries to behave prettily, her instincts rise up against social restrictions. Determination defines Scarlett and drives her to achieve everything she desires by any means necessary. This determination first manifests itself in her narcissistic and sometimes backstabbing efforts to excite the admiration of every young man in the neighborhood. Later, under threat of starvation and even death, she is determined to survive and does so by picking cotton, running her entire plantation, forging a successful business, and even killing a man.

Scarlett also aims to win Ashley Wilkes, and her failure to do so guides the plot of the novel. Ashley's marriage to Melanie Hamilton and rejection of Scarlett drive nearly all of Scarlett's important subsequent decisions. Scarlett marries Charles Hamilton to hurt Ashley, stays by Melanie's side through the war because she promises Ashley she will, and loses her true love, Rhett Butler, because of her persistent desire to win Ashley.

Scarlett possesses remarkable talent for business and leadership. She recovers her father's plantation, Tara, after the war leaves it decimated, and she achieves great success with her sawmill in Atlanta. Despite her sharp intelligence, however, she has almost no ability to understand the motivations and feelings of herself or others. Scarlett lives her life rationally: she decides what constitutes success, finds the most effective means to succeed, and does not consider concepts like honor and kindness. She often professes to see no other choices than the ones she makes.

Scarlett's development precisely mirrors the development of the South. She changes from spoiled teenager to hard-working widow to wealthy opportunist, reflecting the South's change from leisure

society to besieged nation to compromised survivor. Scarlett embodies both Old and New South. She clings to Ashley, who symbolizes the idealized lost world of chivalry and manners, but she adapts wonderfully to the harsh and opportunistic world of the New South, ultimately clinging to dangerous Rhett, who, like Scarlett, symbolizes the combination of old and new.

RHETT BUTLER

Dark, dashing, and scandalous, Rhett Butler brings excitement to Scarlett's life and encourages her impulse to change and succeed. Thrown out of both West Point and his aristocratic Charleston family for dishonorable behavior, Rhett, like Scarlett, goes after what he wants and refuses to take 'no' for an answer. He earns his fortune through professional gambling, wartime blockade-running, and food speculation, behavior that earns him the contempt and even hatred of what he terms the Old Guard—the old Southern aristocracy. Rhett sees through hypocrisy and self-delusion, horrifying people by cutting down their egos and illusions with agility and pleasure.

Whereas Ashley cannot face reality and change, Rhett thrives on both. Because of his opportunism, Rhett symbolizes the New South. However, as the novel progresses, we see that Rhett does care about the Old South. At two critical points in the novel, Rhett abandons Scarlett to commit himself to the Old South. First, he leaves Scarlett in hostile territory and joins the Confederate army. Second, at the end of the novel he leaves Scarlett and goes in search of remnants of the Old South. This sentimentality complicates Rhett's character and reveals that he is partially motivated by emotion. Ultimately, Rhett symbolizes pragmatism, the practical acceptance of the reality that the South must face in order to survive in a changed world. He understands that the U.S. government has overhauled the Southern economy and that the old way of life is gone forever. He adapts to the situation masterfully, but he does not fully abandon the idealized Southern past.

Rhett falls in love with Scarlett, but, despite their eventual marriage, their relationship never succeeds because of Scarlett's obsession with Ashley and Rhett's reluctance to express his feelings. Because Rhett knows that Scarlett scorns men she can win easily, Rhett refuses to show her she was won him. He mocks her, argues with her, and eventually resorts to cruelty and indifference in order to win her. But his fondness for her is evident in his support of her, as he encourages her to shun social customs and gives her money to start her own business.

ASHLEY WILKES

Blond, dreamy, and honorable, Ashley Wilkes is the foil to Rhett's dark, realistic opportunism. Ashley courts Scarlett but marries Melanie Hamilton, thus setting in motion Scarlett's central conflict. Ashley is the perfect prewar Southern gentleman: he excels at hunting and riding, takes pleasure in the arts, and comes from an excellent family.

Scarlett's idealization of Ashley slowly fades as time goes on, and she finally sees that the Ashley she loves is not a real man but a man embellished and adorned by her imagination. Ashley admits to his love for Scarlett, but as a gentleman he ignores this love in order to marry Melanie, the more socially appropriate match for him. He excels at battle despite his doubts about the Southern cause. As the novel progresses, though, Ashley displays signs of weakness and incompetence. After the war he is worthless on the plantation and cannot adjust to the new world. Whereas Rhett and Scarlett survive by sacrificing their commitment to tradition, Ashley cannot or will not allow himself to thrive in a changed society. He sinks even lower as he sacrifices his honor—the only thing he still values in himself—by accepting charity from Scarlett in the form of a share in her mill and by kissing her twice.

Ashley represents the Old South and Southern nostalgia for the prewar days. He epitomizes the old lifestyle and cannot function in the New South that emerges during and after the war. Scarlett clings to him like many Southerners cling to dreams of their old lives, but her eventual recognition of Ashley's weakness and incompetence enables her to see that dreaming of a lost world makes one weak.

CHARACTER ANALYSIS

Themes, Motifs & Symbols

Themes

Themes are the fundamental and often universal ideas explored in a literary work.

The Transformation of Southern Culture

Gone with the Wind is both a romance and a meditation on the changes that swept the American South in the 1860s. The novel begins in 1861, in the days before the Civil War, and ends in 1871, after the Democrats regain power in Georgia. The South changes completely during the intervening years, and Mitchell's novel illustrates the struggles of the Southern people who live through the Civil War era.

The novel opens in prewar Georgia, where tradition, chivalry, and pride thrive. As the Civil War begins, the setting shifts to Atlanta, where the war causes the breakdown of traditional gender roles and power structures. When the South loses the war and the slaves are freed, putting a stop to the Southern way of life, the internal conflict intensifies. White men fear black men, Southerners hate profiteering or domineering Northerners, and impoverished aristocrats resent the newly rich. Mitchell's main characters embody the conflicting impulses of the South. Ashley stands for the Old South; nostalgic and unable to change, he weakens and fades. Rhett, on the other hand, opportunistic and realistic, thrives by planting one foot in the Old South and one foot in the New, sometimes even defending the Yankees.

Overcoming Adversity with Willpower

Scarlett manages to overcome adversity through brute strength of will. She emerges as a feminist heroine because she relies on herself alone and survives the Civil War and Reconstruction unaided. She rebuilds Tara after the Yankee invasion and works her way up in the new political order, taking care of helpless family members and friends along the way. Mitchell suggests that overcoming adversity sometimes requires ruthlessness. Scarlett becomes a cruel business-woman and a domineering wife, willingly coarsening herself in order to succeed. Other characters succeed by exercising willpower, among them Old Miss Fontaine, who watched Indians scalp her entire family as a child and then gritted her teeth and worked to raise her own family and run a plantation. Rhett Butler also wills his way to success, although he covers up his bullheaded willpower with a layer of ease and carelessness.

THE IMPORTANCE OF LAND

In Chapter II, Gerald tells Scarlett that "[l]and is the only thing in the world that amounts to anything." At critical junctures Scarlett usually remembers that land, specifically Tara, is the only thing that matters to her. When Scarlett escapes to Tara from Atlanta during the war, she lies sick and weak in the garden at neighboring Twelve Oaks and the earth feels "soft and comfortable as a pillow" against her cheek. After feeling the comfort of the land, she resolves to look forward and continue the struggle with newfound vigor. Scarlett prizes land even over love. When Ashley rejects Scarlett's proposed affair, he gives her a clump of Tara's dirt and reminds her that she loves Tara more than she loves him. Feeling the dirt in her hand, Scarlett realizes that Ashley is right. At the end of the novel, when all else is lost, Scarlett thinks of Tara and finds strength and comfort in its enduring presence.

MOTIFS

Motifs are recurring structures, contrasts, or literary devices that can help to develop and inform the text's major themes.

FEMALE INTELLIGENCE AND CAPABILITY

Despite the severe gender inequality of their time, women in *Gone with the Wind* show strength and intelligence that equals or bests the strength and intelligence of men. Scarlett is cunning, and manipulates men with ease. She runs Tara when her father falls ill, and eventually realizes that she has a better head for business than most men. She becomes a very successful mill owner, running every aspect of the business and putting her weak, incompetent husband to shame. Melanie, although she is a subdued figure, exhibits increasing strength as the novel progresses, and she eventually emerges as the novel's strongest female character. She provides much of Scarlett's strength, although Scarlett realizes this only at the end of the novel. Melanie also protects Ashley from the world he cannot face. Despite her humble means, she single-handedly facilitates the restoration of Atlanta society. Old Miss Fontaine and Ellen also demonstrate strength and intelligence. Both women act as head of the family, and the narrator describes Ellen as the true mind and strength behind Tara.

ALCOHOL ABUSE

Alcohol abuse occurs throughout the novel, as Gerald, Scarlett, and Rhett all rely heavily on drinking. Characters use alcohol to cope with stress, but when they abuse alcohol, disaster ensues. Drinking is partly responsible for Gerald's death: he rides his horse while drunk, misses a jump, and is thrown to his death. Mitchell suggests that Scarlett cheapens herself unnecessarily by drinking. Gerald disapproves of her drinking, which begins only after she escapes Atlanta, because ladies never drink liquor in polite Southern society. Scarlett continues to drink at Tara whenever she feels overworked or troubled, and she brings her habit to Atlanta when she moves back. Rhett's drinking reveals his insecurity, a disaster for Rhett since he is obsessed with mastery and self-sufficiency. Rhett begins to drink heavily as his relationship with Scarlett deteriorates, and he drinks even more when their daughter, Bonnie, dies.

PROSTITUTION

Prostitution threatens and embarrasses the characters, but it also intrigues them. Scarlett first sees a prostitute in Atlanta and is instantly fascinated. The woman she sees is Belle Watling, and the fascination she feels persists throughout the novel. Belle is an exaggerated version of Scarlett, which perhaps explains Scarlett's interest in her. Both women ignore social mandates, manipulate and seduce men, and trade sex for money. Scarlett offers to prostitute herself to Rhett in order to get money for taxes, putting herself in Belle's moral camp. If Scarlett can be read as a high-class prostitute, Belle can be read as a low-class aristocrat. Belle has the ideal aristocrat's impulse to help the needy; she saves Atlanta's Ku Klux Klan members from prosecution by providing an alibi for them. Mitchell depicts Belle as human and generous and perhaps morally superior to the ruthless Scarlett she resembles.

SYMBOLS

Symbols are objects, characters, figures, or colors used to represent abstract ideas or concepts.

RHETT BUTLER

Rhett represents the uneasy coexistence of the Old South, the New South, and the North. He is nostalgic about the traditional values of the Old South, he is opportunistic and ethically loose in the New South, and he supports the Yankees when he believes in them or when an alliance with the North benefits him. Because he does not ally himself with only one camp, he feels free to criticize all groups, even those he sometimes supports. In his shifting allegiance he symbolizes the uncertainty about the future that pervades the South in the postwar era.

ATLANTA

Atlanta, burned by the Yankees and then rebuilt, symbolizes the resiliency of the South. Atlanta has little to do with the Old South—born as a railroad hub, it becomes strategically vital to the South during the Civil War. After rebuilding, Atlanta becomes a city of the New South, run by Northerners and Scalawags (white Southerners who supported the efforts of the Reconstruction-era government) and is characterized by garish wealth on one side and squalid poverty on the other. Mitchell contrasts this vibrant New South city of saloons, Yankees, and freed slaves with Tara, the Old South plantation that runs on tradition.

Summary & Analysis

Part One: Chapters I–IV

Summary: Chapter I

Sixteen-year-old Scarlett O'Hara lounges on the front porch of Tara, her father's plantation in northern Georgia, in the spring of 1861. She flirts with the nineteen-year-old twin brothers Brent and Stuart Tarleton. The boys excitedly discuss the rumors that a war will soon break out between the North and the South. Scarlett changes the subject to the next day's barbecue and ball at the Twelve Oaks plantation. Brent and Stuart tell her that Ashley Wilkes, the son of the proprietor of Twelve Oaks, will announce his engagement to Melanie Hamilton, his cousin, at the ball. Scarlett, who wants Ashley for herself, tries to act normally but cannot maintain her vivaciousness. The twins leave, baffled by Scarlett's sudden silence.

Summary: Chapter II

> *Land is the only thing in the world that amounts to anything. . .*
>
> (See QUOTATIONS, p. 63)

Distressed by the news of Ashley's engagement, Scarlett hurries to the road to wait for her father, who has gone visiting at Twelve Oaks. Gerald O'Hara rides into view at breakneck speed and jumps a fence. Scarlett teasingly reminds him that he promised her mother, Ellen, not to jump fences, but she vows to keep his reckless behavior a secret. At Scarlett's probing, Gerald confirms that Ashley plans to marry Melanie. He sharply warns Scarlett that she and Ashley would make a terrible match. Gerald says the Wilkeses are too interested in music and poetry, and though Ashley excels at masculine pursuits like riding and shooting, his heart is not in them. On the porch, Scarlett and her father encounter Ellen, who is rushing out to help baptize Emmie Slattery's dying newborn. Mammy, an old slave who has been with Ellen since childhood, does not think Ellen should help the unwed Emmie, whose "white trash" family lives adjacent to the O'Hara plantation.

19

SUMMARY: CHAPTER III

Scarlett thinks about her mother's gentle grace and good breeding, so different from her own willful and passionate ways. Scarlett inherited her temperament from Gerald, who fled his unremarkable life in Ireland after killing another man in a feud. Gerald won his first slave, Pork, and his plantation in a poker game. Though lacking good breeding, Gerald won over the neighbors' hearts with his kindness. Ellen, a placid, serious woman from the aristocratic Robillard family of Savannah, agreed to marry Gerald after the death of her first love, her cousin Philippe. She blamed her family for driving Philippe away from Savannah and from her, and out of frustration and revenge she married the low-class Gerald. Scarlett, the oldest and most strong-willed O'Hara daughter, lacks beauty. Still, she has learned ladylike behavior from Ellen and Mammy and has used her charms to become the most-pursued belle in the neighborhood.

SUMMARY: CHAPTER IV

That day, Gerald has purchased a slave named Dilcey from Twelve Oaks so that Dilcey can be with Pork, who is her husband. At dinner that night, Dilcey thanks Gerald and offers Prissy, her daughter, to be Scarlett's personal maid. Ellen returns late from the Slattery's house. As Ellen leads the nightly prayer, Scarlett concocts a plan to win Ashley from Melanie. She resolves to tell Ashley she loves him at the barbecue. She feels sure that when Ashley knows her true feelings he will elope with her. Scarlett overhears Ellen telling Gerald that Jonas Wilkerson, Tara's Yankee overseer, must be dismissed. Scarlett realizes that Wilkerson was the father of Emmie Slattery's dead child.

ANALYSIS: CHAPTERS I–IV

The first chapters of *Gone with the Wind* present the pre-Civil War South. The O'Haras and the Wilkeses are upper-class, wealthy, white plantation owners who mix traditional values like chivalry, honor, and propriety with a pioneer-style enthusiasm for drinking, horseback riding, and shooting. Family and money rule the social hierarchy, as we see by the neighbors' initial hesitancy to accept Gerald O'Hara. Even so, Gerald's ultimate acceptance by the neighbors shows that a devotion to the South and to its culture—along with a good marriage—can secure respect for a self-made man such as he. The slaves also live in a set social order. House workers outrank field hands and take pride in their higher status. For poor whites like the Slatterys, called "white trash" by wealthy whites and poor slaves alike, survival depends on the charity of rich neighbors. Pride permeates even the lowest rungs of society, however, and the Slatterys refuse to be bought out of their land. The characters also take great pride in the South, and in the weeks before the war this pride swells among the young men who have signed up to fight against the North.

The Southern society of the novel expects men and women to conform to specific gender roles. The narrator notes that the man owns the property but the woman manages it; the man takes credit for managing the property, and the woman then "praise[s] his cleverness." Owning property gives men rights and power, but they share little of the reward that results from the women's hard work. Women have all the work and responsibility of running the property, but enjoy only those rights that men deign to grant them. The narrator stresses the absurdity of these gender roles, sarcastically saying, "[t]he man roared like a bull when a splinter was in his finger, and the woman muffled the moans of childbirth, lest she disturb him." In this society, men expect women to suppress their needs and desires and focus attention on the men. Women are not even allowed to take credit for their own intelligence, bravery, and strength.

Society punishes those women who put a toe over the gender lines. Scarlett, willful like her father, who sometimes treats her like the son he never had, constantly butts against these rigid gender roles. As a child she prefers playing in the trees with boys to sitting calmly inside with girls. As she grows older, she resents putting on a façade of helplessness and silliness to attract men. Like the men of the Old South, Scarlett acts selfishly and vainly and requires constant pampering. Although in character Scarlett resembles the men around her more than she resembles the women, her world does not allow her to budge from the restrictive role prescribed for women. Scarlett adapts to this social restraint, using her cunning and will to present a ladylike face to the world while maintaining her masculine interior.

Foreshadowing abounds in the early chapters. When we see Ellen O'Hara rush off to help Emmie Slattery and Emmie's dying newborn, we glimpse a character trait in Ellen—her selflessness—that becomes significant during the war. Similarly, Gerald's reckless fence-jumping establishes a pattern of dangerous behavior that recurs in a later scene. The brief mention of an implied relationship between the stereotyped characters Jonas Wilkerson, the Yankee overseer, and Emmie Slattery, a poor "white trash" girl, foreshadows these characters' eventual return to the lives of the O'Hara family. These scenes and interactions seem unimportant, but they lend crucial credibility to later plot developments.

CHAPTERS V–VII

SUMMARY: CHAPTER V

On the morning of the Wilkes's party Scarlett chooses a dress that will show off her seventeen-inch waist. Mammy persuades Scarlett to eat something to discourage an unladylike appetite at the barbecue. Ellen cannot attend the barbeque because she must go over the plantation accounts with Jonas Wilkerson before he leaves Tara. On the road, the O'Haras meet the Tarleton women. Gerald and feisty Mrs. Tarleton talk about horses and the possibility of war. Scarlett barely listens, and even the mention of Ashley's engagement fails to disrupt her daydreams of eloping with him.

SUMMARY: CHAPTER VI

All the county's best families have arrived at Twelve Oaks. Scarlett notices a tall, dark, and powerfully built man staring at her without proper deference. His boldness thrills and shocks her. She learns that he is Rhett Butler, a scandalous man from an aristocratic family in Charleston, South Carolina. Rhett once took a girl out without a chaperone and then refused to marry her, though he should have married her after such outrageous behavior. In defense of his sister's honor, the girl's brother challenged Rhett to a duel. Rhett killed the brother during the duel.

Scarlett commands the largest circle of suitors and admirers at the barbeque, including Charles Hamilton. Charles, Melanie's timid brother, showers Scarlett with awkward attention. He even proposes to her, although he is already Honey Wilkes's beau. Scarlett hardly hears Charles, fixing her attention on Ashley. Sitting with Melanie, he seems oblivious to Scarlett's admirers.

The talk of war has attracted men young and old, who boast that they will defeat the Yankees in a month or less. Rhett contemptuously interjects that there are no cannon factories in the South, only a few iron foundries, and no naval power to keep the Southern ports open. He claims that the Yankees will prevail easily and excuses himself before the outraged men can respond.

After the women and girls go upstairs to take their afternoon naps, Scarlett slips into the dark library to intercept Ashley. When Ashley enters, Scarlett confesses her love. To her dismay, he says that he plans to marry Melanie and tells her that she would come to hate him if they were married because they are too different to make a good match. Her pride stung, Scarlett slaps him. He walks quietly out of the room and she hurls a bowl at the wall, shattering it. Unbeknownst to Scarlett, Rhett has been lying on the couch, and he now he sits up and teases her about her unladylike manner. Furious and humiliated, Scarlett storms out with all the dignity she can muster. She goes upstairs and overhears Honey jealously telling Melanie that Scarlett is "fast." To Scarlett's disgust, Melanie, who can see only the good in people, defends Scarlett. Scarlett runs back downstairs just as news arrives that President Lincoln has called for troops, signaling the start of the Civil War. Charles spots Scarlett and again asks her to marry him. Seeing an opportunity to hurt Ashley and Honey and salvage her own pride, Scarlett accepts.

SUMMARY: CHAPTER VII

The next months pass in a blur. Scarlett and Charles marry just one day before Melanie and Ashley's wedding. The men then go off to war and Charles dies of measles only two months later. Scarlett gives birth to a son and names him Wade Hampton Hamilton, after Charles's commanding officer. Scarlett hates the restrictive and boring life of a widowed mother, hates the general excitement over the war, and hates that Ashley is married. She takes a trip to Atlanta to stay with Melanie and her aunt, Pittypat.

ANALYSIS: CHAPTERS V–VII

Rhett Butler appears in Chapter VI as a foil (a character whose attitudes or emotions contrast with and thereby accentuate those of another character) for Ashley Hamilton. Rhett plays the North to Ashley's South, and the contrast between the two men deepens our understanding of the clashing cultural attitudes and tensions in the South. Blond, gentle Ashley stands for the romantic and doomed values of the Southern world, while dark, powerful Rhett represents the hardened, practical Northern world that rises up victorious after the war. When Scarlett desperately attempts to get Ashley's attention, his chivalrous devotion to Melanie contrasts with Rhett's ungentlemanly, heated stares at Scarlett. After Ashley takes Scarlett's slap with dignified pain and sorrow, Rhett mercilessly teases Scarlett in manner unbecoming a refined Southern gentleman.

Scarlett's interactions with Ashley and Rhett mirror the conflict the South is to undergo between old and new ways. The Civil War breaks out just as Scarlett loses Ashley to Melanie. Marrying Ashley, who represents the pinnacle of Southern chivalry, would have cemented Scarlett in the wealthy plantation lifestyle. The declaration of war necessitates the pair of hasty marriages and Scarlett's loss of Ashley. Scarlett's loss of Ashley therefore reflects the South's impending loss of its aristocratic culture in the war. Ashley becomes unattainable for Scarlett, just as the life he represents becomes irrecoverable for the South. At this crucial moment, the introduction of Rhett, an outcast from aristocratic society, represents a new future for both Scarlett and the South. Scarlett, with her desire for more personal freedom than her culture allows her, finds herself drawn to Rhett. Later, Scarlett finds herself struggling to choose between the honorable Southern gentleman Ashley Wilkes and the opportunistic, irreverent cynic Rhett Butler, just as the South finds itself struggling to choose between its traditional culture and values based on land, inheritance, and slave-driven agriculture, and the new Northern way of life driven by the industrial economy and individual freedom.

The omniscient narrative voice shifts between a focus on Scarlett and a general perspective. Primarily, the narrative concerns itself with Scarlett's actions and thoughts, allowing us to see her as other characters cannot. Upon Charles's death, Melanie and Aunt Pittypat think that Scarlett is crying over the loss of her husband, but the narrator reveals that Scarlett is actually crying because of her secret passion for Ashley and her jealous hatred of Melanie. This shifting narrative voice also allows Mitchell to explain historical events that Scarlett does not understand and does not want to understand. It is important to understand the historical context of the novel's setting, which shapes the lives of all of the characters. The narration also speaks from a general perspective in order to illustrate the difference between the sentiments typical of the wealthy Southern culture and those of Scarlett, which are often atypical. For example, when talk turns to war or patriotism, the narrator shows both typical Southern war fever and Scarlett's unusual lack of interest. Shifting between viewpoints accentuates Scarlett's independence.

PART TWO: CHAPTERS VIII–XI

SUMMARY: CHAPTER VIII

On a May morning in 1862, Scarlett, Prissy, and Wade arrive in Atlanta to visit Melanie and Aunt Pittypat. Atlanta, a railroad hub, has sprouted army departments, hospitals, and foundries during the war. At the Hamilton house on Peachtree Street, Pittypat and Melanie are thrilled to see Scarlett. Uncle Henry, Pittypat's brother, talks to Scarlett about Charles's fortune, which is now Scarlett's. The hustle and energy revive Scarlett. Her only complaint is that she must do volunteer nursing work in the soldiers' hospitals, which are full of sweaty, wounded men that stink of gangrene.

SUMMARY: CHAPTER IX

The hospital holds a fundraising bazaar, but as a widow in mourning Scarlett cannot attend without breaching decorum. Unlike the other widows, she thinks it unfair that she works like a "field hand" to prepare for the bazaar but cannot attend. At the last moment, Scarlett and Melanie are called in to work at a booth. At the bazaar, Scarlett is shocked by her own lack of patriotism during the speeches about the glorious Confederate cause. She longs to dance. Rhett Butler, now a famous blockade-runner for the South, appears and teases her about her marriage to Charles. Dr. Meade, Atlanta's foremost citizen, sends around a collection basket to encourage women to donate their jewelry. Scarlett donates her hated wedding ring. Melanie mistakes Scarlett's action for courage and throws her own wedding ring into the basket.

Dr. Meade scandalously proposes that gentlemen must bid to dance with the lady of their choice in order to raise money for the hospital. As a widow, Scarlett is strictly forbidden to dance, but Rhett bids a hundred and fifty dollars in gold on her. To the shock of the crowd, Scarlett accepts and hurries to the dance floor. Rhett tells Scarlett that he admires her beauty and spirit and that he knows the Cause bores her as it bores him. Scarlett pretends to be angry, but she knows that what he says is true.

SUMMARY: CHAPTER X

The next morning, Atlanta buzzes with gossip about Scarlett's shocking behavior. Pittypat says that Rhett is a terrible man, but forgives him when he sends a gift: Melanie's wedding ring, which he bought back. Gerald arrives to confront Rhett and take Scarlett back to Tara in disgrace. He leaves to talk to Rhett and returns in the middle of the night, drunk and penniless from playing poker. In the morning, Scarlett promises to keep his behavior a secret as long as he allows her to stay in Atlanta. He agrees.

SUMMARY: CHAPTER XI
The following week, Scarlett sneaks into Melanie's room to read a letter Melanie recently received from Ashley. In it Ashley discusses his doubts about the war, but Scarlett pays little attention to his soul-searching questions. She is simply relieved that Ashley has not written Melanie a love letter. Scarlett puts away the letter, convinced that Ashley still loves her.

ANALYSIS: CHAPTERS VIII–XI
Mitchell divides *Gone with the Wind* into sixty-three chapters, dividing those chapters into five parts. Each new part begins with a shift in Scarlett's life and in the life of the South. Chapter VIII, the first chapter of Part Two, marks the end of Scarlett's comfortable and privileged life at Tara and the beginning of her consciousness of the Civil War. Though the war actually starts in Chapter VII, Scarlett does not move to Atlanta until Chapter VIII, and it is only in Atlanta that she begins to feel the reality of the war. Part Two also marks the beginning of Scarlett's life as a seventeen-year-old widow. Earlier, back at Tara, gala parties and masses of admirers surround her. In Atlanta her social life changes entirely. Although Scarlett knows some people in Atlanta, she now spends her time with Melanie, Pittypat, and older married or widowed women.

The Civil War relaxes the stringent rules governing women's behavior, however. Because men must go off to war, courtship and marriage must happen with new speed. The hospitals need volunteers so badly that even widows like Scarlett find themselves attending to wounded and sick men and seeing sights previously thought too vulgar for a woman's eyes. Even guidelines for widows change slightly. According to the customs of the Old South, widows must wear black for years after the death of their husbands, and for them it is unthinkable to enjoy the company of an unmarried man, much less dance with one. However, the topsy-turvy atmosphere of war makes such rules mutable, and thus Scarlett can dance with Rhett in Chapter XII and afterward still show her face in Atlanta society. In a time of few resources and overwhelming motivation to support the war effort, people realign their priorities to give primacy to the war rather than to custom.

Just as Mitchell uses Ashley and Rhett to represent the Old South and the New South, respectively, she equates Tara with the Old South and Atlanta with the changing, New South. Tara stands for a slavery-driven plantation world of leisure and luxury for the wealthy owners. Atlanta, Gerald tells Scarlett, was born the same year she was, and like Scarlett it lives through newness and change. Scarlett's old way of life cannot survive in this new world. No longer idle and pampered as she is back at Tara, she spends much of her time nursing wounded soldiers and rolling bandages for the war. She even notes that she feels like a slave. In Scarlett's eyes, at least, social codes have been turned on their heads when a Southern belle like herself must work as hard as a field hand. At Tara, Scarlett tries to adhere to old Southern values. In Atlanta, however, she begins to defy the rules that society has impressed upon her since birth. Scarlett has always felt rebellious, but in Atlanta she acts on her rebelliousness, boldly dancing despite her widowhood. Scarlett remains nervous about stepping out of line, but Atlanta's wartime culture grants her room to express her strong will and follow her selfish desires—until Atlanta itself changes in Part Three.

CHAPTERS XII-XVI

SUMMARY: CHAPTER XII

The war drags on. Port blockades make food, clothing, and other necessities increasingly difficult to obtain. Rhett is the most famous Confederate blockade-runner, sneaking boats through the Yankee blockade in order to sell cotton and other Southern products in exchange for necessities. He becomes the most popular man in town despite his reputation for disregarding social customs. He calls on Scarlett frequently, and she quickly abandons any pretense of mourning Charles's death. She enjoys the informality occasioned by the war and lives an active social life. After months of polite behavior, Rhett starts publicly expressing his contempt for Confederate idealism and declares that he works for personal gain, not for the Southern cause. One night at a party, Rhett scandalizes his audience by exclaiming that the war is about money, not pride, rights, or glory. In the carriage ride home, Melanie defends Rhett, revealing that in his letters Ashley has expressed beliefs similar to Rhett's. The revelation that her shining idol and a scoundrel have the same opinions about the war confuses Scarlett.

SUMMARY: CHAPTER XIII
The entire city, with the exception of the Hamilton household, vilifies Rhett. He continues to call on Scarlett, however, and gives her a fancy hat from Paris so she will stop wearing the required black mourning veil. One day Melanie tells Scarlett that a prostitute named Belle Watling gave her a considerable sum of money for the hospital. Belle wrapped the money in a handkerchief, which Melanie now holds, and Scarlett sees that it bears Rhett's initials. Shocked that Rhett would consort with a prostitute, Scarlett flings the handkerchief into the fire.

SUMMARY: CHAPTER XIV
The people remain optimistic despite food shortages, death, illness, and poverty. The Confederacy has won important battles, and rumors begin to circulate that the war will be settled at an impending battle at Gettysburg, Pennsylvania. As the battle begins, news of widespread casualties slowly trickles back to Atlanta. A large crowd of women gathers before the newspaper office to wait for casualty lists. Melanie, Scarlett, and Pittypat learn that Ashley has survived, but nearly every family in Atlanta has lost a relative in the fighting. Stuart and Brent Tarleton have died.

SUMMARY: CHAPTER XV
The Confederacy loses the battle at Gettysburg. At Christmastime, Ashley comes home on a brief leave of absence. Scarlett loves seeing him, but wishes she could speak to him alone. Just before he leaves, she gets a moment with him. Ashley asks Scarlett to look after Melanie if he is killed. Scarlett quickly agrees and then kisses him passionately. Ashley kisses her back but quickly breaks away as Scarlett proclaims her love, and he hurries to the train station looking agonized.

SUMMARY: CHAPTER XVI
It is early in 1864. The Confederate army has lost ground and Atlanta suffers from cold and hunger. Atlanta openly reviles Rhett as a food speculator and a profiteer. Scarlett receives two devastating pieces of news: Ashley has been captured, and Melanie is preg-

nant. Rhett has learned of Ashley's imprisonment and tells Scarlett that Ashley could have won his freedom by betraying the Confederacy. Scarlett asks why Ashley would have refused such an opportunity, and Rhett, who claims he himself would have accepted, replies contemptuously that Ashley is too much of a gentleman.

ANALYSIS: CHAPTERS XII-XVI

Rhett, as a symbol of the New South, forces the people around him to listen to the harsh truths about the war, pointing out the economic problems that Southern leaders refuse to acknowledge. Although he is abrasive and contemptuous, Rhett cuts through the rosy rhetoric of leaders like Dr. Meade and exposes the hypocrisies and weaknesses obscured by the South's rampant patriotism. Rhett insists on voicing truths that the South would rather not face. He asserts that the war is more about money than people will admit and that those who make grand speeches about states' rights care for nothing but their own wealth and privilege. Ashley also recognizes the truths that Rhett voices, but, as Scarlett realizes, Ashley nevertheless resigns himself to fighting for a lost cause. Ashley reinforces his position as symbol of the Old South, fighting desperately for a life that has already been lost to the New South that Rhett Butler represents.

Until the Civil War, the Southern economy depended largely on its cotton production, which relied on slave labor for the intensive work. The slave-driven economy brought great wealth to the plantation owners and left the South relatively untouched by the industrial revolution that swept the North. The South became dependent on the North and on England to buy its crops and to supply manufactured goods. As Rhett explains to the men at Twelve Oaks, the South has raw resources but lacks means of production. When the North blocks off Southern ports, the South finds its markets cut off. It can neither export its crops for income nor import goods for consumption. Blockade-runners like Rhett become invaluable as a way of getting and selling goods. As the blockade tightens, the entire South suffers from a shortage of goods and skyrocketing prices.

Those people who control resources—government contractors and blockade-runners like Rhett—soon win the public's ire by profiting from the scarcity of goods. The people who control the goods can control the prices. Because goods are so scarce, demand rises, and people like Rhett can push prices to astronomical heights, sometimes even holding onto goods instead of selling them right away so that prices go up still more. Southerners initially bless the blockade-runners for procuring goods, but as they begin to understand the reality of price-fixing, their praise turns to hatred. The profiteering of the blockade-runners marks the beginning of the South's helplessness, which continues with the postwar descent of the carpetbaggers, Northerners who go down South to profit under Reconstruction-era policies.

Some critics fault Mitchell's novel for focusing entirely on the upper classes, glorifying Southern culture and glossing over its faults. Mitchell paints a picture of a South victimized by greed and selfishness. For example, she portrays the plantation owners as helpless in the face of the profiteer's opportunism. She condemns hypocritical government contractors and the Southerners who stay in the local militia instead of going into battle farther north. Other inhabitants of the South seem to exist in a harmless, happy world. Mitchell suggests that their only sin is naiveté. However, portraying wealthy Southerners as victims of profiteering ignores the history of how the plantation owners accumulated the wealth of which they soon found themselves stripped. Gerald, a self-made man, gets his plantation through a poker game, but his success, like the success of every plantation owner in the South, depends upon the exploitation of slaves and the crowding out of poor whites like the Slatterys. Neither the plantation owners nor Mitchell acknowledge the fact that most rich Southerners succeed by oppressing people. Consistent with the sentiments of her time and class, Mitchell acknowledges only the wrongs committed against the upper class.

PART THREE: CHAPTERS XVII–XX

SUMMARY: CHAPTER XVII

By May of 1864, General Sherman's Yankee army has fought its way into Georgia and is dangerously close to Atlanta. Rhett infuriates Dr. Meade by declaring that the Confederacy will not hold the Yankees back. Everyone in Atlanta clings to a faith in the Confederacy. As the war creeps closer, the trains deliver wounded and dying soldiers by the thousands. Scarlett feels that she can no longer bear her work and sneaks away from the hospital. She encounters Rhett, who is impeccably dressed despite the wartime scarcity. He drives her back to Peachtree Street. On the way, they encounter a group of marching slaves, and Scarlett recognizes Big Sam, the old foreman at Tara. He tells her proudly that the slaves are being sent to dig trenches for the gentlemen and women to hide in when the Yankees come. Scarlett knows that they are really digging the trenches for the Confederate army to fight off the Yankees. Rhett drives on and teases Scarlett about how she must secretly want him to kiss her. He says he does not make advances toward her because she childishly clings to her love for Ashley. Scarlett becomes so angry that she makes Rhett stop the carriage and let her out.

SUMMARY: CHAPTER XVIII

Atlanta is under siege, and even old men and young boys are called upon to fight. John Wilkes, Ashley's elderly father, joins the militia. Gerald stays home only because of his bad knee. The Yankees outnumber the Confederates, and dying soldiers pour into the city, collapsing on lawns and crowding into houses. The citizens of Atlanta begin to flee in panic, and Pittypat joins the exodus to Macon. Scarlett longs to go home to Tara, but she must remain with Melanie, who is too pregnant to relocate. Scarlett knows nothing about childbirth, but Prissy says that she has helped with many deliveries.

SUMMARY: CHAPTER XIX

The Yankees sever all rail lines but one. Shells hammer Atlanta. Scarlett is frantic and Melanie lies in bed sick. Uncle Henry stops by on a leave of absence to tell Scarlett that John Wilkes has been killed. Rhett finds Scarlett crying on her porch. He tells her that he likes her but does not love her and asks if she will become his mistress. Scarlett storms upstairs furiously.

SUMMARY: CHAPTER XX

After thirty days of siege, quiet falls. The Yankees move to capture the Jonesboro rail line, which lies very near Tara. Scarlett's terror grows when she receives a letter from Gerald saying that Ellen and both of Scarlett's sisters have typhoid fever. By the first of September, Scarlett does not know whether the Yankees are at Tara or whether her family is still alive. She longs to go home, but she will not break her promise to Ashley by leaving Melanie. Melanie tells Scarlett the baby will come very soon and makes Scarlett promise to take the baby if Melanie dies.

ANALYSIS: CHAPTERS XVII–XX

Throughout Part Two, Mitchell builds suspense by focusing on the war as it inches closer to Atlanta. She describes every new development in the war, which begins to take on central importance in the lives of the characters. When the battle at Gettysburg begins, the characters and the narrator start paying closer attention to news of the war. Nearly every family Scarlett knows loses a relative, and she herself knows many of the boys who die. After the battle of Gettysburg, the war takes a decisive turn in favor of the Yankees, and the old carefree optimism fades from Atlanta. The city runs short on food and clothing. Scarlett, once so blithely ignorant about the war, now feels surrounded by its effects. Ashley is captured, and masses of injured men fill the hospital where Scarlett works—she cannot escape the war's horrors. Mitchell shows us the war as Scarlett sees it, describing the progress of the conflict but never depicting a single battle scene.

In 1864, Ulysses S. Grant, the commanding general of the Union army, dispatched General William Tecumseh Sherman with a force of 100,000 men to topple the last stronghold of the Confederacy, the relatively untouched states of Georgia and the Carolinas. After conquering Atlanta, Sherman set out on his famous march "from Atlanta to the sea." During his march, Sherman broke the backbone of Confederate resistance and paved the way for Northern victory. Sherman, who is also credited with the saying "War is hell," considered it his duty not merely to defeat the Confederate army but to crush the South beyond repair. As a result, his troops waged economic warfare against the people they conquered, destroying property, confiscating food and livestock, burning crops and houses, and damaging railroad systems. This scorched-earth campaign won Sherman a fearsome reputation throughout the South. The characters in *Gone with the Wind* circulate many horror stories about Yankees, accusing them of rape, dismemberment, and burning. Their stories reflect the ravages wrought by Sherman's commitment to all-out destruction.

Even though Rhett insists that he does not love Scarlett, his romantic interest in her becomes increasingly evident. Rhett realizes that Scarlett is stuck in Atlanta looking after a woman she despises, and he teases her about this morbidly humorous situation. Rhett's nonchalance and mockery infuriate Scarlett and wound her pride, but Rhett intrigues her. She and Rhett share many of the same shockingly unconventional views, although only Rhett admits them. Rhett belittles prominent Atlanta figures whom Scarlett secretly despises, and he speaks frankly about the lack of Southern patriotism, a lack that Scarlett notices as well. Rhett sees through Scarlett's artifice and knows she shares his unpopular opinions. Rhett knows that Scarlett's girlish flirtations hide a selfish heart, a perception that leaves Scarlett powerless to control him as she controls other men. She despises him, but she also wants to win him. Mitchell shows us Rhett's confidence, sense of humor, and intelligence, and we begin to wonder whether Rhett is the evil tempter everyone thinks him or the perfect match for Scarlett.

CHAPTERS XXI–XXV

SUMMARY: CHAPTER XXI
The defeated Confederate army abandons Atlanta and retreats south, leaving the city to the Yankees. Scarlett goes to the depot to find Dr. Meade and encounters a seemingly endless trail of dead and dying soldiers. Dr. Meade cannot leave them to help Melanie, and everyone else is evacuating the city. Melanie goes into labor, and Prissy admits to Scarlett that she lied when she claimed to know how to deliver a baby. For the first time in her life, Scarlett strikes a slave, slapping Prissy across the face. Scarlett hurries to try to help Melanie.

SUMMARY: CHAPTER XXII
After a long, painful labor, Melanie gives birth to a boy. Atlanta is nearly deserted, but Scarlett sends Prissy to find Rhett and tell him to come help them escape to Tara.

SUMMARY: CHAPTER XXIII
Confederate soldiers confiscate Rhett's horse and carriage, but he steals an old horse and cart and drives away with the women, Wade, and the baby. The retreating Confederate army has torched Atlanta's foundries and storehouses to keep the Yankees from looting them. Scarlett feels unutterably grateful for Rhett's strength and protection as they ride through the blazing streets. At last they make it out of Atlanta, and Scarlett repeats her desire to go to Tara. Rhett says that to do so would be suicidal, as the woods near Tara are full of Yankees. To Scarlett's shock, Rhett announces that he is abandoning her to join the Confederate army. He kisses Scarlett passion-

ately, overwhelming her with unfamiliar feelings. Her fury at his announcement quickly returns, though, and she slaps him. He walks away, and Scarlett takes the reins.

SUMMARY: CHAPTER XXIV

The next morning, Scarlett finds herself in pain after a long night of driving and sleeping in the woods. Melanie seems near death, and Scarlett whips the sickly horse back onto the road. Scarlett longs for the comfort of her mother and Tara. They pass the neighboring manors, all empty and burned, but find Tara still standing. Gerald greets Scarlett with the news that Ellen died the previous day. Scarlett's sisters are still sick with typhoid fever. Gerald seems like a helpless old man, so Scarlett takes charge. Gerald tells her that the Yankees used Tara as a headquarters and have ravaged the plantation, stripping it of food. Dilcey recently gave birth, so she nurses Melanie's child. Mammy seems to lack strength and confidence without Ellen, and Dilcey tells Scarlett that the Yankees have burned all the cotton and that Ellen died crying the name "Philippe." Scarlett drinks some whiskey and sinks into despair. She remembers her proud family history and thinks of her ancestors who overcame hardships and won fortunes. Feeling strengthened by their example, Scarlett falls into a peaceful, drunken sleep.

SUMMARY: CHAPTER XXV

Scarlett wakes in the morning with a headache. She realizes that Gerald, who seemed merely weary the previous night, is suffering from dementia and does not understand that Ellen is dead. Scarlett goes to Twelve Oaks to search for food and finds old turnips and cabbages. As she eyes the torched remains of the once-great plantation, she resolves to look forward rather than backward and vows to herself, "I'm never going to be hungry again." The war soon fades from Scarlett's mind as she devotes herself to feeding the hungry mouths at Tara, tending to the three sick girls, and struggling to stay afloat. Scarlett hardens and grows sharp-tongued under the strain and worry of being in charge, but she gains strength from her deep connection to Tara and her passion to hold on to the land.

ANALYSIS: CHAPTERS XXI–XXV

Scarlett's whiskey-induced flashback to her ancestors' struggles illustrates the power of the human will to overcome even the most severe adversity. Mitchell's flashback technique, though less than subtle, reminds us that Scarlett's situation is not unique and that she must fall back on the human capacity to meet unthinkable challenges. Other characters also exhibit strength of will and help guide Scarlett's actions. As a child, Old Miss Fontaine witnessed the scalping of her entire family and survived. She recognizes the survival instinct in Scarlett and gives Scarlett advice based upon her own experiences. Rhett was thrown out of his house without a penny, but he manages to amass great wealth. Melanie gives birth almost unaided but never relinquishes her optimism. She exhibits incredible strength by doing hard work despite her physical weakness. Scarlett, Rhett, and Melanie could not be more different from one another, but they all possess wells of strength, and Mitchell celebrates their ability to survive the most difficult ordeals.

When Rhett abandons Scarlett to join the Confederate Army, it marks a turning point for both of them. Rhett's steadfastly anti-Southern exterior begins to crack, revealing that he may turn out to be a hero not just for the New South but for the Old South as well. Rhett's brash anti-South rhetoric loses strength until finally he decides to join the Confederate army. Never the shining knight, however, Rhett performs his patriotic duty while leaving Scarlett in the dust to save herself and the lives of four others. Scarlett has only a horse, a carriage, and her own wits, and she has never driven a carriage before. However, she grits her teeth and maneuvers safely past soldiers of both camps who would gladly rob her of her horse. The long ride is harrowing, but Scarlett has changed so much that she can handle the difficulty. When she arrives at Tara, she finds herself caring for her demented father and the bewildered Mammy.

Scarlett would gladly give up her new responsibility and collapse into the arms of her mother, but Ellen has died. Scarlett cannot put down the burden that she never meant to pick up. In order to persevere, she adopts a mantra that returns throughout the novel: "I'll think about it tomorrow." Scarlett uses this phrase to explain and justify her decisions. She convinces herself that she must act without thinking about her actions or her plight. This mantra becomes her survival mechanism. When she feels she must do something unethical, she repeats her mantra and does what she must in order to protect Tara, her own life, and the lives of those people in her care. Ignoring her conscience comes easily to Scarlett. She routinely ignores her moral twinges when, for example, she reads Ashley's letter to Melanie. Still, the acts she must now commit are not naughty but ruthless, and she often finds herself repeating her mantra during her difficult days at Tara.

Gerald's dementia results from the loss of Ellen, whom he loved dearly. His dementia symbolizes the inability of the Old South to recover and adjust after the Civil War. Gerald cannot run his plantation, comprehend the new order of things, or accept the loss of his wife and his way of life. He embodies the helpless state of the postwar South. Like many of his peers, he must rely on others to take care of him and make decisions for him. Scarlett takes loving charge of him, but other men in Gerald's position find themselves at the mercy of opportunists from the North. Men like Gerald, who have known only the easy, good life of the Old South, find themselves bereft after the Civil War.

CHAPTERS XXVI–XXX

SUMMARY: CHAPTER XXVI
One day a Yankee cavalryman rides up to Tara and enters the house with his pistol drawn, looking for loot. Scarlett shoots him point-blank with Charles's pistol. As he falls down dead, she sees Melanie at the top of the stairs carrying Charles's sword. For the first time, Scarlett feels admiration for Melanie. They discover money in the Yankee's pockets. Though shocked by the thought that she has killed, Scarlett feels justified in defending Tara and happy to have the Yankee's precious money and horse.

Scarlett visits the nearby Fontaine plantation and finds the women eager to share their meager supplies. Scarlett tells her troubles to Old Miss Fontaine, who warns Scarlett to save something to fear lest she become too cold and hardened. To Scarlett's chagrin, Old Miss Fontaine says that at one point in her life she picked cotton to support her father and she never considered herself white trash for doing so. Scarlett returns to Tara and takes up the work of picking cotton, which she considers humiliating "slave work." Only Dilcey helps her. Mammy and Pork insist that, as house workers, they will not perform field hand labor. Melanie is still too weak for laboring. Still, now that she has food, money, and a horse, Scarlett believes the worst is over.

SUMMARY: CHAPTER XXVII

In mid-November the family learns that the Yankee army is again marching toward Tara. Terrified of losing the food and the house, Scarlett sends everyone into the swamp to hide with the animals and the food. She keeps Melanie's baby with her. Scarlett refuses to abandon Tara and meets the Yankees at the front door. A swarm of soldiers pours in around her, destroying everything they do not steal. One soldier tries to take Wade's grandfather's sword, which is now Wade's birthright, but Scarlett persuades the Yankee sergeant to stop him. The enraged soldier runs into the kitchen and sets the place on fire as the Yankees stream out of the house. With great effort, Scarlett and Melanie succeed in putting out the fire. Scarlett's contempt for Melanie once again gives way to grudging admiration.

SUMMARY: CHAPTER XXVIII

Around Christmastime, a man named Frank Kennedy and a few Confederate soldiers visit Tara, looking for food for the army. Frank tells Scarlett and Melanie that General Sherman has burned Atlanta to the ground, although Aunt Pittypat's house escaped the destruction. Frank confides in Scarlett that the end is near, and he finally becomes engaged to Scarlett's sister Suellen after years of courtship.

SUMMARY: CHAPTER XXIX

By April the war is over, and Scarlett, relieved rather than dejected, makes plans to plant cotton for next year's market. The roads are safe once again, and neighbors help each other get back on their feet.

SUMMARY: CHAPTER XXX

Streams of returning Confederate soldiers begin passing through Tara, and Scarlett grudgingly offers them hospitality, sharing Tara and her food with them. A soldier named Will Benteen, a working-class Georgian with a wooden leg, stays on to help with the plantation. He is a godsend, quietly and competently assisting with the land. He falls in love with Scarlett's sister Carreen, whose devotion to her prayer books and memories of Brent Tarleton prevent her from noticing Will's attentions. One day, Uncle Peter, a slave, comes from Aunt Pittypat's house with a letter from Ashley. Ashley is alive and walking home from Illinois. Anxious weeks pass, and Ashley finally arrives. Melanie runs down the front path to meet him and Scarlett starts to run after her, but Will grabs her skirt to stop her. He gently reminds her that Ashley is Melanie's husband.

ANALYSIS: CHAPTERS XXVI–XXX

Scarlett must adapt quickly to keep pace with the quick changes facing the South. Starvation, the chaos of the war, and the lack of help transform Scarlett from a spoiled coquette into a hardened woman. She stoops to levels she could never have imagined in her old life. Although she adapts, however, Scarlett does not really change. She simply gives free reign to the tendencies once considered shamefully unladylike. In some ways, Scarlett has always had a personality ideally suited to disaster. Her old cunning and selfishness now serve her well, and by developing traits she always possessed she becomes completely self-sufficient and competent. Because Scarlett has never held to the standards of the old times, she has no trouble dropping them now. She is determined to "change with changing ways," as Old Miss Fontaine puts it. Scarlett and Rhett stand out among the novel's Southern characters for their chameleon-like ability to adapt to a new set of conventions.

During the hard months at Tara, Melanie becomes mentally stronger, and we start to see her as an alternative heroine to Scarlett. Melanie retains her kind heart, timidity, and physical frailty, but she gains a quiet, fiery determination. She helps Scarlett put out the fire set by the Yankee, and, in one of the novel's most memorable scenes, tries to defend Tara against the Yankee thief by wielding a sword too heavy for her to lift. Melanie is just as brave as Scarlett, enduring the same hardships and exhibiting the same steely determination to survive, but Melanie's bravery is untarnished by the selfishness and ruthlessness that drive Scarlett. Melanie's belief in helping others and in maintaining Southern values motivates her heroic actions. Mitchell suggests that Melanie possesses a more worthy breed of heroism than Scarlett does, but she also suggests that because Melanie lacks Scarlett's nastiness she will not survive the new order. Like Ashley, Melanie represents the Old South, a South that cannot survive in the post–Civil War era. The weakening of Melanie's body parallels the weakening of the South. As Melanie becomes sick during pregnancy in Atlanta, Atlanta becomes sick. As Melanie totters around Tara, Atlanta struggles to stay alive. Despite their struggles, however, both Melanie and the South maintain their pride and gentility.

Mitchell's use of derogatory terms for specific ethnic or socioeconomic groups causes many readers discomfort. Throughout the novel, white characters and black house slaves refers to field hands as "darkies," "niggers," and "free-issue trash." Poor whites are labeled "white trash" and "crackers." Many of these racist and classist terms, offensive though they may be, were part of the common language of the time period in which the novel is set. Mitchell researched her novel meticulously, and in order to paint a true-to-life picture, she used the idiom of the Old South. However, while historical accuracy can explain some characters' use of this language, historical accuracy does not compel the house slave Pork to talk of "trashy niggers." Pork uses this language solely to denounce other black people. Surely a self-hating individual such as Pork could have existed in the Civil War South, but Mitchell fails to depict such an individual's more numerous counterparts, who hated the torture they suffered at the hands of white oppressors, and who longed to regain their dignity.

The slaves depicted in *Gone with the Wind*, especially the freed slaves, are stereotypes rather than real people. Historically, some slaves remained loyal to their white owners after the Civil War, but many of them left to find the freedom they had long been denied. Mitchell thus paints an unrealistic picture when she writes that not a single house servant deserts Tara. Mitchell buys in to the white party line of the Civil War era, which held that slaves loved and needed their masters. In this novel slaves profess overwhelming and unrealistic loyalty to white families. For instance, in Chapter XVII, Big Sam digs trenches with pride because he thinks he is helping gentle white people to hide. Mitchell makes Big Sam not only loyal to his slave-owners but also naïve and childish, and therefore in need of white guidance and support. Mitchell also stereotypes slaves as dishonest, having Prissy, for example, lie about having experience delivering babies. *Gone with the Wind* contains multiple derogatory descriptions of blacks; it perpetuates negative stereotypes rather than investigating the black position in the South at the time of the Civil War.

PART FOUR: CHAPTERS XXXI–XXXIV

SUMMARY: CHAPTER XXXI

*The people who have brains and courage come
through and the ones who haven't are winnowed out.*
(See QUOTATIONS, p. 64)

Will returns from a trip to Jonesboro with terrible news: the Scalawags and carpetbaggers have raised the taxes on Tara. Scarlett
does not have enough money to pay the taxes, so she goes to ask
Ashley for advice. He says he cannot help her. With self-loathing,
he tells Scarlett he cannot bear to face reality; he misses the Old
South. Scarlett tells Ashley that she still loves him and suddenly
asks him to escape with her. They kiss passionately, and Ashley
tells Scarlett that he loves her but cannot leave Melanie, for he
loves his honor more than he loves Scarlett. Placing a clump of
Tara's red clay in Scarlett's hands, Ashley tells Scarlett that he
knows she loves Tara even more than she loves him. Scarlett
remembers her passion for Tara and walks back to the house, vow-
ing never to throw herself at Ashley again.

SUMMARY: CHAPTER XXXII

Jonas Wilkerson, the former overseer of Tara who now works for
the Freedmen's Bureau, and Emmie Slattery arrive at Tara dressed
in opulent finery. Wilkerson announces his intention to buy the
plantation for Emmie, and Scarlett realizes that he is the man
responsible for raising the taxes on Tara to drive the O'Haras
away. She curses the visitors and orders them to leave. Wilkerson
snidely tells Scarlett that she is no longer high and mighty. Scarlett
spits at him as he drives away in his fancy carriage. Desperate,
Scarlett decides to go to Atlanta to try to marry Rhett Butler. The
thought of marriage to Rhett repulses her, but she has heard of his
vast funds, which he reportedly stole from the Confederate trea-
sury. Scarlett cannot seduce Rhett looking ragged and poor, but
there is no money for a new dress, so she makes one out of Ellen's
fine green velvet curtains. She decides that if Rhett does not want
to marry her, she will offer to become his mistress if he will save
Tara. Mammy agrees to help make the dress, on the condition that
Scarlett let her act as chaperone.

SUMMARY: CHAPTER XXXIII

Scarlett and Mammy arrive to find Atlanta burned nearly beyond recognition. The streets teem with blue-coated Yankee soldiers and freed slaves. At Aunt Pittypat's house, Scarlett hears of the downfall of nearly all the prominent families in Atlanta. Rhett Butler has been sent to jail for allegedly killing a black man who insulted a white woman. Scarlett is so surprised that she scarcely hears Aunt Pittypat ask her whether the newly formed Ku Klux Klan is active around Tara.

SUMMARY: CHAPTER XXXIV

The next morning, Scarlett visits Rhett in prison. She pretends to be well off and tries to seduce him. She nearly succeeds, but he notices the calluses on her overworked hands and guesses her true reasons for coming to see him. He refuses her blunt offer to be his mistress and tells her that he even if he wanted to give her money, the Yankees would trace any draft he wrote and confiscate all his wealth. Rhett tells her mockingly that she can attend his hanging, and she leaves filled with bitterness and shame.

ANALYSIS: CHAPTERS XXXI–XXXIV

After the Civil War ends, the events of the novel take place during the era of Reconstruction. Reconstruction was the transitional period during which the Southern states were rebuilt under a new government and new laws. When the war ended, the Northern-controlled Congress refused to grant seats to newly elected congressmen from the South and took full control of the Reconstruction process. The South felt shamed and helpless, forced to live under what it perceived as foreign rule by the North. For Scarlett and her friends, Reconstruction proves more painful than the war itself. During the war, even the most painful losses in battle are made bearable by the spirit of rebellion. After the war, however, defeat sours everyone. The South can no longer take pride or comfort in its spirit of rebellion.

Three types of people dominate the novel's portrayal of Reconstruction: Republican officials, Northerners in a South that was solidly Democratic; Scalawags, Southerners who traitorously supported the Republican Party after the war; and carpetbaggers, Northerners who came to the South after the war in search of power and profit. The old hierarchy turned upside down when

Congress denied the right to vote to many Southerners who participated in the war and quickly granted suffrage to black men. The Republican governments in the South, led by Scalawags and carpetbaggers, rode roughshod over the once-mighty plantation owners and aristocrats of the South. Scarlett's friends resent the power of the Freedmen's Bureau, the federal agency designed to protect the interests of freed slaves, whom the Southerners view as ignorant and incompetent. Scarlett herself confronts the power of the government when her old employee Jonas Wilkerson, employed at the local Freedman's Bureau, easily manipulates the tax code to increase the taxes on Tara illegally in the hope of obtaining the plantation for himself.

Mitchell suggests that there are two choices for Southerners living under Reconstruction: they can cling to their gentility and pride and do as they are told, or they can fight back. Ashley, too moral to behave with the necessary cunning, clings to his old Southern gentlemanly ways. Scarlett, on the other hand, is prepared to abandon all the social ideals from before the war in order to save Tara. Before the fall of Atlanta she throws Rhett out of her house for proposing that she become his mistress, disgusted by his affront to her honor. Now, however, she rides to Atlanta willing to become his mistress in exchange for the three hundred dollars she needs, prioritizing matters of survival over matters of honor. Like all other Southerners, Scarlett suffers her share of shame and helplessness in the postwar years.

Scarlett changes after her last proclamation of love to Ashley. He rebuffs her once again, and finally she leaves behind the last of her spoiled, coquettish ways. She cannot understand Ashley's self-loathing and passivity or his unwillingness to act on his love for her. She finally comprehends, however, that his integrity will always prevent him from leaving Melanie. Scarlett realizes that "[t]he words, hospitality and loyalty and honor, meant more to him than she did," and that passion and flirtation will not win him. For the first time, she imagines herself in Ashley's position and realizes that it pains him that they cannot act on their attraction. After her conversation with Ashley, Scarlett makes Tara the driving force in her life, which complements her resolution never to throw herself at Ashley again. She has abandoned all trace of her foolish girlhood and has become a woman on a mission.

Chapters XXXV–XXXVIII

Summary: Chapter XXXV

Trudging dejectedly from Rhett's jail cell, Scarlett encounters Frank Kennedy in a new buggy. Frank says that he now owns a store and plans to buy a sawmill soon, which would be extremely profitable because of all the rebuilding needed in Atlanta. Despite Frank's engagement to Suellen, Scarlett determines that she must marry Frank in order to pay the taxes on Tara. She tells Frank that Suellen is set to marry another man. Scarlett realizes that, contrary to most well-bred Southerners, she would rather have money than pride.

Summary: Chapter XXXVI

> *A startling thought this, that a woman could handle business matters as well as or better than a man...*
> (See QUOTATIONS, p. 65)

Two weeks later, Frank marries Scarlett and gives her the money to save Tara. Scarlett ignores Suellen's sadness and the neighbors' malicious gossip. She manipulates Frank into making more profitable business decisions, fending off guilt with her practice of putting off worrying about things. Frank soon falls ill, and Scarlett takes advantage of his immobility, going to the store to see the account books. She quickly realizes that Frank runs the business badly—his friends owe him vast sums of money that he is too embarrassed to collect. Scarlett thinks she could do a much better job in the strictly male world of business and begins to think of acquiring a sawmill.

Rhett, who has blackmailed his way out of jail, enters the store and congratulates Scarlett on her marriage. After mocking her for still loving Ashley, Rhett changes his tone and agrees to loan her the money to buy the sawmill as long as she does not use the money to help Ashley.

To Frank's chagrin, Scarlett quickly becomes a ruthless businesswoman, devoting all her time to the mill and turning a sizable profit by any means necessary. Scarlett is the only businesswoman in Atlanta, and the city gossips disapprovingly. Embarrassed and afraid of his wife, Frank hopes that a baby will take Scarlett's mind off business.

SUMMARY: CHAPTER XXXVII

Tony Fontaine, a planter's son from Scarlett's county, arrives one night in a panic. He has killed Jonas Wilkerson and a black man. He explains that Wilkerson was telling freed slaves they have the right to rape white women, and one such slave made a lewd comment to Tony's sister-in-law. Ashley, who accompanied Tony on his revenge mission, advised him to seek help from Scarlett and Frank. Tony leaves, and Scarlett reflects that the South has become a dangerous place. She begins to fear losing everything to the powerful Yankee government and freed slaves, and she pins all her hopes for safety on making money. She tells Frank that she is pregnant. While Frank glows with pride and relief, Scarlett thinks of the Ku Klux Klan, a newly formed organization supposedly intended to protect whites against violent blacks. She feels grateful that Frank is not in the Klan because the government in the North has been gearing up to crush the organization.

SUMMARY: CHAPTER XXXVIII

Scarlett searches for the right man to run the mill while the birth and the baby occupy her. To the horror of old Atlanta, she also begins doing business with the Yankees, although she hates them. She shakes with anger when three Yankee women declare in front of Uncle Peter that blacks are untrustworthy. Scarlett begins to run into Rhett frequently, and she drinks brandy to soothe her nerves. News arrives that Gerald is dead, and Scarlett heads home with a heavy heart.

ANALYSIS: CHAPTERS XXXV–XXXVIII

Scarlett's return to Atlanta to marry Frank Kennedy begins a new stage in the novel, and her emergence as a ruthless businesswoman begins a new stage in the development of her character as a strong, independent woman. People in Atlanta describe Scarlett's head for business as masculine or unladylike, but, despite criticism, Scarlett drives ahead and proves herself more business-savvy than any man in the novel except Rhett. Frank feels emasculated and embarrassed by Scarlett's success, but he is too weak-willed to stop her. Only Rhett does not disapprove of Scarlett's decision to enter the business world. As Scarlett becomes more independent, she feels drawn to Rhett because he talks business with her and respects the business-savvy facet of her character. With her newly discovered business acumen, Scarlett finds herself in an unlikely alliance with Rhett. They share an unabashed instinct for self-preservation that nearly everyone around them lacks. Scarlett's business savvy also brings her into further contact with Yankee businessmen and paves the way for her movement into Yankee social circles.

The brief scene depicting Tony Fontaine's escape raises the tense issue of race relations in the era after the war. We see evidence of the violence of this relationship earlier in Rhett's arrest for allegedly killing a black man who insulted a white woman. Historically, freed slaves (often referred to as "free-issue" blacks in the novel) lacked resources, education, property, and self-direction, and white Northerners manipulated them in an effort to shore up political power. The bulk of the freed slaves found shelter in squalid, hastily built shantytowns. Mitchell ignores these facts, however—one of the novel's most blatant exhibitions of racism. She describes black people's lives as "a never-ending picnic" and attributes their hardships to their inability to care for themselves once away from the plantation owners' care. She describes freed slaves as "creatures of small intelligence" who take "perverse pleasure in destruction." The only blacks not portrayed as part of a threatening, insolent mass are loyal house servants like Mammy and Pork, who never once indicate any dissatisfaction with their lowly position. The novel doesn't make any acknowledgment that unhappy house slaves even existed, nor does it hint at the terrible and terrifying power of slave-owners over their slaves. Rather, it portrays a world in which slaves are always a beloved part of the family, and no one strikes them except the brutal Scarlett.

Mitchell's racism reveals the mindset of Southern gentleman like Ashley Wilkes. Terrified by their sudden loss of political and social power, such men fixed blame on blacks. Confused by a world of freed slaves, they became convinced that black men posed a sexual threat to white women, and formed the Ku Klux Klan to protect their wives and to feel important and powerful once again. Mitchell does point to the Klan's danger and foolishness, but she mitigates her condemnation of the group by showing only peaceful Klan participants. Even though Ashley supports the Klan, he opposes the organization on principle and is "against violence of any sort." Thus Mitchell suggests that men like Ashley join the immoral Klan on moral grounds and thus cannot be faulted for their membership if they refrain from violence. According to Mitchell, they remain unsullied by the Klan's evil as long as they stick fast to their own principles. Mitchell's demeaning depiction of blacks and her neutrality about the Ku Klux Klan demonstrate that racism pervaded not only Scarlett's time but also Mitchell's.

CHAPTERS XXXIX–XLII

SUMMARY: CHAPTER XXXIX

Scarlett returns to Tara for Gerald's funeral. Will Benteen tells her that Suellen, desperate for more money, tried to trick Gerald into taking the oath of loyalty to the Union. Men who swear loyalty to the Union receive compensation for property lost during the war. Will says that Suellen got Gerald drunk and got him to agree to sign anything. Although drunk, Gerald realized what was about to happen and ripped up the oath. He mounted his horse and rode away. When he tried to jump a fence, his horse pitched him off, killing him upon impact. Will shocks Scarlett by telling her that he plans to marry Suellen so that he can stay at Tara forever.

SUMMARY: CHAPTER XL

When she sees Tara, Scarlett's heart surges with love. Ashley performs the funeral service and Will asks to say a few words. To keep any of the mourners from criticizing Suellen, Will announces their engagement and asks that no one else speak after him. Old Miss Fontaine tells Scarlett that the secret to success lies in changing with the changing times, rising up after misfortune, and using people and then discarding them. Scarlett finds the speech confusing and dull.

SUMMARY: CHAPTER XLI

After the funeral, Scarlett gives Gerald's gold watch to Pork as a reward for his faithful service. Upon learning that Ashley intends to move to New York with Melanie, Scarlett appeals to him to take a half-interest in the mill and live in Atlanta. Ashley refuses, ashamed to live on her charity and tormented by his love for Scarlett. When Scarlett begins to cry, Melanie rushes into the room. She learns of Scarlett's offer and urges Ashley to accept it in order to repay Scarlett's kindness and let Beau grow up in Atlanta rather than in the hostile North. Ashley accepts the offer at the expense of his honor.

After Suellen and Will's wedding, Carreen enters a convent, and Ashley, Melanie, and Beau move into a little house in Atlanta adjacent to Aunt Pittypat's house. Melanie's optimism, generosity, and adherence to old Southern values make her house the social nucleus for proud Southern families. Ashley proves incompetent at wringing profits from the labor of the freed slaves, so Scarlett announces her intention to lease convicts to work in her mills.

SUMMARY: CHAPTER XLII

Scarlett gives birth to an ugly baby girl and names her Ella Lorena. Scarlett is desperate to get back to the mill, but Frank forbids her to return. Atlanta has become dangerous, and Frank worries for Scarlett's safety. The Yankees, he says, are trying to root out the Ku Klux Klan, and anger has begun to brew among the freed slaves in areas like Shantytown. A one-legged, one-eyed mountain man named Archie begins to work as Scarlett's escort into town. Rude and intimidating, Archie quickly becomes an Atlanta institution, chaperoning women around town. When Archie hears about Scarlett's plan to lease convicts to work in the mills, he threatens to stop assisting her. He tells her he was a convict for forty years after murdering his adulterous wife, and says that convict leasing is worse than slave ownership.

Scarlett learns that the Georgia legislature has refused to ratify a Constitutional amendment granting blacks citizenship. Though many Southerners take pride in the legislature's resolve, Scarlett realizes it will make the Yankees even harder on Atlanta. She leases ten convicts to work in her mills, hiring a Yankee Irishman named Johnnie Gallegher as their foreman. Atlanta is appalled at Scarlett's actions, and Archie quits as promised, but Gallegher gets an astonishing amount of work out of his men. To Scarlett's dismay, Gallegher fares far better than Ashley as a manager.

ANALYSIS: CHAPTERS XXXIX–XLII

Despite the Northerners' efforts to crush Southern society through Reconstruction, the South slowly rebuilds itself. Many characters marry, often in matches that would have been unthinkable in the days before the war. Suellen's marriage to the poor white man Will Benteen is such a match. In prewar times, a poor man like Will would not have dreamed of wooing a landed, high-class woman like Suellen. Atlanta's aristocracy begins to reestablish its social network, using Melanie's house as a meeting place. The physical rebuilding of Atlanta proceeds rapidly, as Scarlett's success with the lumber mill illustrates. Postwar life is difficult, but it goes on—

even matriarchs take on small business projects, and Confederate army veterans who were listless and despondent after the war begin working feverishly to rebuild their fortunes. Southerners remain almost defiant. Gerald's death strikes a note of Southern pride and resolve, for he goes to his death hating the Yankees and defying them. The spirit of his defiance seems to echo throughout Georgia and the South during Reconstruction, as the Georgia legislature's stubborn refusal to ratify the amendment granting citizenship to blacks demonstrates.

Will Benteen emerges as the only poor white character whom Mitchell develops fully. He is a real person, not simply a sketch or a symbol. Other non-aristocratic characters, such as Emmie Slattery, the "white trash" character, and Jonas Wilkerson, the evil Yankee, never develop into anything more than stereotypes. Will, however, becomes a part of the O'Hara family and Scarlett's trusted advisor. As a "cracker" (a lower-class white), Will has only a few slaves and little property before the war, a serious handicap to one's status in a society that measures worth and class by the amount of land and slaves a man possesses. Before the war, the O'Haras would never have dreamed of socializing with Will, let alone allowing him to marry into their family. But with Tara in ruins, the O'Haras welcome Will's help. He arrives at just the right moment to earn their respect and favor. Once Will gets his foot in the door, his good Southern manners win over the entire family and he successfully jumps class boundaries. With so many men killed in the war, the South must make class boundaries more permeable in order to survive. Still, class boundaries do not collapse completely: though Will advances in the Atlanta social scene, he does so not by his own merits but by marrying into an aristocratic family. Additionally, both Scarlett and the narrator exhibit a contemptuous attitude toward Emmie. Emmie's family has next to nothing, and the South rejects her. Desirous of moving up in the world, Emmie must leave the South and join Northern society in order to improve her social lot.

Scarlett's decision to lease convicts illustrates the extent to which she has changed into a cutthroat businesswoman. Before the war, Scarlett would have been horrified, or at least would have feigned horror, at the mere mention of convicts. Now she hires them as workers. Everyone, even Archie, a convicted murderer, considers Scarlett's decision inhumane. Convicts are not protected as free workers are, and they are treated badly by the people who lease them, sometimes dying from the abusive working conditions. Scarlett has never cared much about the consequences of her actions, thinking almost exclusively about how great a profit will result from them. She proceeds with the plan to hire convicts over the chorus of objections. Her ruthlessness reaches new heights during this difficult economic time, which suggests not only Scarlett's inhumanity but also the general cruelty practiced by both Northerners and Southerners after the Civil War. Scarlett is predisposed to ruthlessness, but she is also a product of ruthless times.

CHAPTERS XLIII–XLVII

SUMMARY: CHAPTER XLIII
Rhett comes to visit and reminds Scarlett that he loaned her the money to buy the mill on condition that she refrain from using the money to help Ashley. Noting that Ashley is now being paid to run the mill, Rhett tells Scarlett she has become unscrupulous. Scarlett insists that she had no choice and says she will be kind once she is rich and secure. Laughing, Rhett tells her to urge Frank to spend more nights at home. Scarlett thinks Rhett is insinuating that Frank is having an affair, but Rhett laughs and departs, leaving Scarlett confused and angry.

SUMMARY: CHAPTER XLIV
By March, Georgia has come under harsh military rule for its refusal to grant the vote to blacks. Tensions mount between the freed blacks, the Confederate whites, the Yankee soldiers, and the Ku Klux Klan. One day, driving through the dangerous black area of Shantytown, Scarlett encounters Big Sam, who is wanted for killing a Yankee. Scarlett decides to help him escape to Tara and tells him to meet her in the same spot that night. She rides to the mill, where she finds that Johnnie Gallegher has been starving and whipping the convicts. She flies into a rage, but Johnnie threatens to quit unless she gives him free reign to do as he pleases. Remembering that he has doubled the mill's productivity, Scarlett lets the matter drop. On her way back through Shantytown, Scarlett is attacked by a poor white man and his black companion. Big Sam appears and fights the attackers. He then jumps into Scarlett's carriage and drives her to safety as she collapses in sobs.

Summary: Chapter XLV

That night, Frank sends Scarlett to Melanie's house while he and Ashley attend a political meeting. At Melanie's, the other women and Archie seem strangely tense. Rhett appears and asks Melanie where Ashley and Frank have gone, saying that it is a matter of life and death. Melanie tells him they have gone to the old Sullivan plantation, and Rhett disappears. Melanie explains to Scarlett that Frank and Ashley are Klansmen, as are all the men they know, and they have gone to avenge the attack on Scarlett.

A Yankee regiment bursts in and demands to know the men's location. At last Rhett, Ashley, and a man named Hugh Elsing stumble in drunkenly. Rhett tells the Yankee captain that he and the other men were at Belle Watling's house all night. The Yankee, a friend of Rhett's, is suspicious but embarrassed, and he quickly departs. Rhett dispatches Archie to burn the Klan robes and dispose of two unspecified dead bodies. Ashley is not drunk but wounded, and Scarlett realizes the whole scene has been a desperate cover-up. In her concern for Ashley, Scarlett hardly notices Frank's absence. Rhett finally informs her that Frank has been shot through the head.

Summary: Chapter XLVI

The next day, a Yankee court calls Belle, Ashley, and Rhett to testify about the events of the preceding evening, and their convincing alibi clears them of all charges. Melanie expresses her gratitude and admiration to Belle, who is dumbstruck that a great lady like Melanie has stooped to speak to a prostitute. The other Confederate women in Atlanta look down on Scarlett for her connection to the preceding evening's events.

Summary: Chapter XLVII

Scarlett sits alone in her bedroom, drinking brandy and feeling sick with guilt. She believes that she manipulated Frank into marrying her and then caused his death. Rhett arrives and proposes to Scarlett. Surprised, Scarlett refuses and tells Rhett that she does not love him. Rhett tells her to marry him for fun. He takes her in his arms and kisses her deeply. Feeling dizzy and faint, Scarlett accepts the proposal. Rhett says he must leave for a long trip but that they will be married when he returns. Atlanta is scandalized to hear about Scarlett's engagement to Rhett, but Scarlett ignores the gossip, marries Rhett, and goes to New Orleans for a long honeymoon.

ANALYSIS: CHAPTERS XLIII–XLVII

In this section, the pervasive influence of the Ku Klux Klan becomes clear. The Klan plays a pivotal role in the lives of many of the novel's most prominent male characters. Now, for the first time, both we and Scarlett begin to understand the extent of Klan involvement among the white men of Atlanta. Scarlett's friends have kept her in the dark about Frank's Klan involvement, knowing that she disapproves of the Klan. Scarlett believes that Frank goes out to political meetings at night, even when Rhett laughingly hints at Frank's Klan membership by urging Scarlett to have Frank spend more nights at home. She remains oblivious to Frank's Klan involvement until the night he is killed. In Chapter XLV, Scarlett's peaceful oblivion shatters when she learns that not only Frank but also Ashley and all the other Southern men she knows, young and old, have joined the Atlanta Klan. No one in Scarlett's circle is untouched by the Klan, because Klansmen will avenge any attacks—real, threatened, or imagined—on them or their women. The Yankees in power keep a watchful eye on the Klansmen, waiting for any chance to jump on them and convict them. When the Klan moves or takes action against people they consider to be enemies, the Klansmen put themselves in great danger. Only Rhett's quick scheming saves the prominent men involved in revenge against Scarlett's attackers.

As a result of the Klan raid, not only does Scarlett lose Frank but she also invokes the wrath of Atlanta. The women of Scarlett's society blame Scarlett for endangering their men. The Klan believes that any attack on a member of that society must be revenged, so if Scarlett provoked the attack then she must be held responsible for whatever happens to the men engaged in the revenge mission. Scarlett already feels guilty about Frank's death, and to be held responsible for the woes of the other women is too much for her to bear. The Atlanta women hate Scarlett because she has apparently endangered Southern men and even gotten some killed, and furthermore because they must now feel grateful to Rhett Butler, whom they detest, and to Belle, whom they scorn. After the raid, Scarlett feels cast out of her society. This feeling partially explains her hasty engagement to Rhett. Although the engagement at first seems selfish, the scorn of Scarlett's society makes it easier and perhaps even comforting for Scarlett to break with this society and marry Rhett, another outcast.

The attack on Scarlett once again illustrates the novel's racist implication that good slaves remain loyal to their masters and freed slaves are always violent and bad. The events are almost cartoonish, as the figure of the bad slave, who accepts his freedom, does evil to Scarlett, while the figure of the good slave, who rejects his freedom, does good for her. The freed slave who attacks Scarlett presumably lives in Shantytown, which the novel depicts as a hotbed of rebelliousness. Big Sam, who saves Scarlett, has just announced that he is tired of freedom and wants to go back to Tara to work for the O'Haras. This desire to leave Shantytown is supposed to demonstrate Big Sam's essential goodness, since he clearly wants no part of the seedy stirrings of the freed slaves. Scarlett's attack is one of many incidents in which Mitchell glorifies slaves like Mammy, Pork, and Uncle Peter who reject freedom in favor of staying with their old masters. She also vilifies slaves who leave their old masters and move to the cities, portraying them as insolent and menacing. While this racism probably reflects the attitudes of whites in Scarlett's time and even in Mitchell's time, it is one of the reasons why blacks and whites protested at theaters across the country when the movie version of *Gone with the Wind* premiered in 1939.

PART FIVE: CHAPTERS XLVIII–LII

SUMMARY: CHAPTER XLVIII
Scarlett and Rhett enjoy a lavish New Orleans honeymoon. On their last night, however, Scarlett has a nightmare: she is running through the mist near Tara, searching for something she cannot name. Rhett comforts her, telling her she will get used to being safe. He adds that she can have as much money as she likes for anything she wants but that he will not spend a cent on her businesses because he does not care to support Ashley Wilkes.

SUMMARY: CHAPTER XLIX
Still angry with Scarlett for causing the Klan raid that endangered so many men, the women of Atlanta intend to cut Scarlett and Rhett out of society. Melanie passionately defends Scarlett and prevents the community from shunning her completely. Scarlett supervises the construction of the most lavish mansion in Atlanta and befriends many wealthy and corrupt Republicans, Scalawags, and carpetbaggers. She loves being rich, and cares little that the society dedicated to the Old South refuses to attend her parties. Rhett pays the bills, though he regards Scarlett's new social circle with undis-

guised contempt. He warns her that she will regret severing ties with Old Atlanta when the Democrats are back in power, but Scarlett dismisses this possibility.

Summary: Chapter L

Scarlett generally enjoys her life with Rhett, though he often mocks her and treats her with indifference. One afternoon, Scarlett discovers, to her horror, that she is pregnant. She wants to terminate the pregnancy, but Rhett angrily says that he once saw a woman die while aborting her baby and refuses to allow Scarlett to risk her life. Scarlett gives birth to a daughter, and Rhett stuns everyone with his unabashed love for his daughter. They name her Eugenie Victoria, but when Melanie observes that the baby's eyes are blue like the bonnie blue flag (a Confederate flag), the baby's nickname becomes Bonnie Blue Butler.

Summary: Chapter LI

Scarlett goes to the mill to go over the books with Ashley. Ashley indicates that he is jealous of Rhett. Thrilled that Ashley still loves her, Scarlett decides to tell Rhett that she wants separate bedrooms, which implies that she wants to end their sexual relationship. Rhett tells her with indifference that he will look elsewhere for female companionship. After he leaves, Scarlett cries while thinking of everything she will miss about sharing a bed with Rhett, like waking in his arms after a nightmare and long conversations before sleep.

Summary: Chapter LII

Rhett decides that Bonnie must not suffer in Atlanta simply because he and Scarlett have fallen from society's grace. He begins an elaborate campaign to regain the good favor of the old Southern matrons. He also breaks ties with the Republican Party and works to put the Democrats in power. Gradually, Old Atlanta comes around and embraces Rhett and Bonnie, though it still scorns Scarlett and her Republican socializing. When she is two years old, Bonnie develops a pronounced fear of the dark. Rhett allows Bonnie to sleep in his room with a lit lamp every night.

Analysis: Chapters XLVIII–LII

Scarlett's pregnancy brings children to the forefront of the novel for the first time. Beginning with Wade's birth in Chapter VII, Scarlett has been a mother for nearly the entire novel. Until now, however, her children do not play an important role in either Scarlett's life or the plot: Wade is not mentioned for long sections of the novel, though he becomes slightly more prominent in Part Five, and Ella receives only passing mention after her birth. Bonnie, however, appears more often in the novel because of Rhett's love for her. Scarlett has never really loved anyone besides her parents—her passion for Ashley is more childhood fantasy than love—so it is not surprising that she does not care for her children. Scarlett's instinct for self-preservation is so strong that it leaves little room for her to worry about the preservation of those to whom she feels no attachment. Each time she becomes pregnant, she reacts with a horror that would have been regarded as highly unnatural in her day. Scarlett exhibits none of the natural maternal thought essential to the feminine nature. Scarlett also dislikes her children because they resemble their fathers instead of her: Wade is timid and weak like Charles, and Ella is ugly and silly like Frank. Scarlett cares little for her husbands, so she cares little for the children of her husbands. Bonnie exhibits the selfishness and strong will that Rhett and Scarlett share, so she elicits feeling from Scarlett just as Rhett does.

In this section, Rhett solidifies his position as the novel's male hero. Throughout the novel, Mitchell makes it difficult for us to embrace Rhett, painting him as charming at times and downright obnoxious at others. Mitchell originally presents Rhett as an anti-Southern opportunist, although she endears him to us through his wit, strength, and charisma. He also charms us by refusing to fall under the spell of Scarlett's charisma. He teases her and torments her about the same qualities that we may find annoying and repellent in Scarlett. In Chapter XXIII Rhett proves that some of his unpatriotic scoffing is just bluster when he joins the Confederate army. Now Rhett becomes even more respectable by supporting the Democrats and becoming a devoted and loving father. Rhett also shows that despite his seeming indifference he does care for Scarlett. He vehemently objects when she wants to endanger her life with a primitive method of abortion. Though Scarlett clings to her childhood passion for Ashley, she comes to rely increasingly on Rhett's strength and love. As he becomes more and more important to Scarlet over the course of the novel, Rhett replaces Ashley as the dominant male figure.

Rhett's decision to change party loyalties foreshadows the coming shift in political power in the South. Rhett, who always caters to the group that is set to emerge wealthy and powerful, now deserts the Scalawags and Republicans to join the Democrats. As the Southern Democrats rebuild their party and the Republicans become increasingly corrupt and unpopular, Rhett transfers his loyalties and his money to the Democratic cause, showing that he cares more about his social position than his honor. He makes this shift for Bonnie's sake, to regain the respect of Southern society, but he does it in accordance with his unerring instincts. Rhett's shrewd political sense never fails, and, as he has sensed it would, Reconstruction soon draws to a close.

CHAPTERS LIII–LVII

SUMMARY: CHAPTER LIII

Melanie throws a surprise birthday party for Ashley, and Scarlett goes to the lumberyard to delay Ashley. Scarlett and Ashley talk wistfully about the old days before the war. Scarlett finally allows herself to look back on old memories and begins to understand that Ashley's unhappiness stems from the loss of the Southern gentleman's way of life. Her passion for Ashley feels dim now, replaced by a friendly, sympathetic love. Scarlett begins to cry and Ashley takes her in his arms to comfort her. Ashley stiffens, and Scarlett turns to see that Archie and India, Ashley's sister, have been watching them.

Archie tells Rhett about the scene. Scarlett, knowing the story will spread, dreads facing the party. Rhett berates her, calls her a coward, and forces her to go to the party. Scarlett realizes that she cares about no one's judgment but Melanie's. When Scarlett enters the party, everyone falls silent and turns to stare. Melanie emerges from the crowd, takes Scarlett's hand, and asks Scarlett to receive the guests with her.

SUMMARY: CHAPTER LIV

That night Scarlett paces frantically in her room, unable to abandon the memory of Melanie's fierce faithfulness to her. She slips downstairs to find some brandy and encounters Rhett, who is drunk and angry. He tells Scarlett that he loves her and that he would kill her if he thought it could take Ashley from her mind. Suddenly Rhett seizes her in his arms and carries her upstairs, tearing her clothes off and kissing her roughly. After a wild night, Scarlett wakes with new passion for Rhett. She is nervous and excited to see Rhett again, but he has left and does not return for several days. He returns and nonchalantly tells her he has been at Belle's. They exchange harsh words, and Rhett tells Scarlett that he is taking Bonnie on a long trip.

SUMMARY: CHAPTER LV
Melanie continues to support Scarlett faithfully and openly breaks with India's camp. All of Atlanta's prominent families choose sides, and the feud splits the town in two, ending Ashley's relationship with India and Melanie's relationship with Aunt Pittypat, in whose house India lives. Scarlett reflects that both she and Ashley must now hide behind Melanie's protective strength.

SUMMARY: CHAPTER LVI
Rhett stays away for three months, and Scarlett misses him terribly. She discovers that she got pregnant the night before Rhett left and for once the news of pregnancy makes her happy. Rhett mocks Scarlett upon returning. She angrily tells him of her pregnancy and he replies, "Cheer up, maybe you'll have a miscarriage." Enraged, Scarlett swings at him. Rhett steps out of the way, and Scarlett falls down a long staircase. As a result of her fall, she loses the baby and nearly dies. Melanie stays by her side. Rhett, frantic with guilt, weeps and tells Melanie that he loves Scarlett and fears that he has killed her with his crazed jealousy.

SUMMARY: CHAPTER LVII
A month later, Scarlett goes to Tara to recuperate. Rhett tells Melanie he wants Ashley to buy the mills from Scarlett. He will anonymously give Ashley the money to make the purchase, and Melanie must encourage Ashley to buy the mills. Hopeful that if Ashley owns the mills Beau might attend Harvard and Scarlett might worry less, Melanie reluctantly agrees. Ashley buys the mills, and the four have a little party to celebrate. But Scarlett denounces Ashley's plan to fire Johnnie Gallegher and send away the convicts. Ashley replies that ill-gotten money cannot make anyone happy. Scarlett protests, but when Rhett asks her sardonically whether her money has made her happy, she falls silent.

ANALYSIS: CHAPTERS LIII–LVII
Scarlett begins to understand her love for Rhett as the novel draws to a close, and Rhett begins to understand his love for Scarlett more

fully. Scarlett's understanding begins with her encounter with Ashley in the lumberyard and consequent realization that she feels only warm friendship for him. Her meeting with him should feel imbued with all of the accumulated, pent-up passion of their years-long hidden love for one another, but instead it feels safe and sad. In Chapter LXII, she realizes she loves Rhett in a revelatory moment, as if finally waking up from a recurring nightmare. Scarlett's feelings for Rhett begin to emerge and surprise her as she starts to understand her own hopes and dreams. At the same time, Rhett's love for Scarlett cracks his sardonic, nonchalant mask. Rhett fully realizes his love for Scarlett only after he treats her horribly. His tumultuous, tightly contained passions break out of his control several times in this section. His jealousy is evident in his claim to Scarlett that he would kill her if it would make her stop thinking about Ashley. His emotions continue along this violent trajectory as he carries Scarlett up the stairs and brutally makes love to her. Rhett confesses all his feelings to Melanie only after insulting Scarlett deeply and causing her to fall down the stairs. The depths of his dark soul are not exposed until it rages and then repents.

The sex scene in Chapter LIV presents difficulties for a reading of the novel that sees *Gone with the Wind* as a feminist work starring a feminist heroine. By modern standards, Rhett rapes Scarlett, or at least practices sadism on her without her consent. Mitchell writes that "he had humbled her, hurt her, used her brutally." If Scarlett were a feminist character, she would be outraged at how Rhett dehumanizes her to satiate his own desires. But Scarlett is not a feminist character, and she reacts to this treatment with elation and "the ecstasy of surrender." Her grateful reaction to Rhett's sexual violence makes Scarlett seem more the wilting woman her society expects and less the strong and independent woman more typical of modern society. Scarlett, whom we usually see emotionally abusing men, now glories in being physically abused by a man. At worst, Mitchell presents rape as a manly last resort, good for winning a difficult woman's respect and love. At best, she presents two characters who make a perfect match, Scarlett's masochism and Rhett's sadism adding up to a mutually satisfying sexual experience.

Mitchell almost certainly intends Scarlett to be seen as a strong, progressive woman throughout the novel, and it seems unlikely that she would intentionally undercut our opinion of Scarlett's strength in the last chapters. Even after submitting to his violent sexual advances, Scarlett continues to defy Rhett feistily. She tries to slap him when he insults her and her unborn child, for example. We may see Scarlett's reaction to Rhett's sexual attack as unsettling, but readers of Mitchell's day might have found it empowering. Scarlett has the agency to enjoy sex in a time when women's sexual pleasure was not discussed. Also, even in Mitchell's time, sex was seen as an obligation in marriage, not a choice, and spousal abuse was not loudly condemned as it is today. Rhett's behavior therefore does not absolutely transgress the boundaries of acceptable married behavior.

As the novel draws toward its climactic moment, its consistent large-scale view of Southern society collapses into a tight focus on Scarlett, Rhett, Ashley, and Melanie. Although *Gone with the Wind* is a historical novel, near its end it becomes most importantly a powerful story about a group of memorable characters, and it puts aside history in favor of a close examination of personal relationships.

Chapters LVIII–LXIII

Summary: Chapter LVIII
Rhett devotes his time and attention to Bonnie and to the Democratic Party. He reveals that he and Ashley disbanded Georgia's Ku Klux Klan by convincing its members that it was counterproductive. By October of 1871, the efforts of men like Rhett and Ashley bring back a Democratic majority in the state legislature, effectively ending Reconstruction.

Summary: Chapter LIX
Bonnie becomes increasingly spoiled, and Rhett does nothing to curb her desires. She likes to ride, so he buys her a little Shetland pony and teaches her to jump obstacles. One day Bonnie asks Rhett for a higher bar, and, against his better judgment, Rhett complies. Her eyes flashing like Gerald's, Bonnie calls out to Scarlett to "watch me take this one!" Remembering her father uttering the same words before his death, Scarlett cries out to Bonnie to stop, but it is too late. The pony misses the jump, throwing Bonnie to her death. Rhett sequesters himself in his room with the dead child, refusing to bury her because of her fear of the dark. Scarlett accuses Rhett of murdering Bonnie, and Rhett responds that Scarlett never cared for Bonnie. Melanie hurries to Rhett's side. She persuades him

to let Bonnie's funeral go forward and sits up all night with Bonnie's body as Rhett sleeps.

SUMMARY: CHAPTER LX

Some weeks after the funeral, Scarlett grows afraid and lonely and wishes Rhett would comfort her, but he is constantly drunk, hostile, and bitter. His physical condition deteriorates and he spends much of his time at Belle Watling's. Scarlett longs to tell him that she does not blame him for Bonnie's death but she cannot approach him. She even longs for the company of her old friends, but she has alienated everyone except Melanie, Ashley, and Aunt Pittypat.

SUMMARY: CHAPTER LXI

Scarlett is in Marietta, Georgia, when she receives an urgent telegram from Rhett saying that Melanie is dying. Scarlett rushes home, where she finds Melanie on her deathbed. Although Melanie was forbidden to have more children because of her frailty, she got pregnant and had a miscarriage, and the effort has doomed her. Suddenly realizing how much strength she has drawn from Melanie over the years, how much Melanie has done to protect her, and how much she has wronged Melanie, Scarlett feels a desperate sense of loss. At Melanie's bedside, Scarlett promises to look after Ashley and Beau. She seeks Ashley to take comfort in his strength, but when she sees him broken and weak, she realizes that she must have loved a fantasy that she created, not the man before her.

SUMMARY: CHAPTER LXII

Scarlett goes outside to clear her head, distraught by the loss of both Melanie and her fantastical love for Ashley. Walking through a thick mist, she realizes with terror that her surroundings exactly mirror those of her recurring nightmare in which she runs through a fog looking for something, not knowing what she hopes to find. She begins to run, and suddenly she realizes that she wants to find Rhett. Immediately she understands that she loves him and that he has loved her all along. No longer afraid and sad, she runs joyfully home to him.

SUMMARY: CHAPTER LXIII

My dear, I don't give a damn.

(See QUOTATIONS, p. 66)

When Scarlett confesses her feelings to Rhett, he tiredly tells her that his love for her has worn out and that he is going away. Unmoved by her passionate pleas, Rhett says he is going to search for a calm, dignified life like the one he and the South lost in the war. Scarlett asks what she will do if he leaves her, and he says their relationship cannot be fixed. He parts with the words, "My dear, I don't give a damn." Scarlett collapses in misery and shock, but suddenly she decides she must go back to Tara. There, she thinks, Mammy will comfort her. Scarlett believes she will recuperate and grow strong again and find a way to win Rhett back, just like the spirited people in the Old South "who would not know defeat, even when it stared them in the face." Scarlett feels comforted and stronger and refuses to think of her pain until tomorrow, falling back on her mantra, "tomorrow is another day."

[T]omorrow is another day.

(See QUOTATIONS, p. 67)

ANALYSIS: CHAPTERS LVIII–LXIII

Bonnie's death climactically links Scarlett's past, present, and future, lending a sense of inevitability to the conclusion of the novel. Because she is their child, Bonnie represents the union between Scarlett and Rhett, and her death symbolizes the death of Scarlett and Rhett's marriage. Bonnie's death also evokes Gerald's death, in Chapter XXXIX, thus infusing the present with a painful reminder of the past. Bonnie dies in exactly the same manner as Gerald, after calling out exactly the same words before taking the fatal jump. Scarlett even notices how closely Bonnie resembles Gerald in the moment before the horse jumps. This look backward heightens the tension of the story, but it also foreshadows the end of the novel. Mitchell shows that Bonnie, like Gerald, dies from her O'Hara hardheadedness. Scarlett ignores this warning that stubborn actions lead to death, however. She has achieved great things throughout the novel by virtue of her willpower, and at the conclusion of the novel she decides to persevere no matter how great the obstacles facing her. As Gerald's death symbolizes not only his hardheaded nature but also his pride in the Old South, the recall of his death at this moment in the novel foreshadows the fact that Scarlett, like her father before her, will persevere in the spirit of the Old South, not just in the spirit of the new order.

At the end of the novel, Scarlett finally understands Ashley and Rhett. She has long perceived the striking similarities between the two men, who often surprise her with shared beliefs in the futility of war, the rampant hypocrisy in the South, and the foolishness of the Ku Klux Klan. Finally she realizes that the crucial difference between them is not that Ashley is fine while Rhett is coarse but that Ashley is weak while Rhett is strong. When Melanie dies, Scarlett feels strength drain from her. She turns to Ashley for support and finally understands that Ashley is not strong. He is a weak man, not the heroic man she imagines him to be in the beginning of the novel. On her way home, she realizes that Rhett is the man who gives her real strength, whereas Ashley only reflects the strength that Scarlett projects onto him.

Scarlett and Rhett torment us with their inability to feel the same emotion at the same time. If one feels passionately in love, the other feels sullen; if one is talkative, the other is silent; if one is desperate, the other is indifferent. They cannot work out their difficulties because they are too similar, and they are both equally to blame for the failure of their love. Scarlett ignores years of Rhett's devotion, too self-absorbed to see that true love lies just underneath Rhett's veneer of apathy. Rhett cannot rein in his passion for Scarlett, and lets it erupt in violence. When he does win her love, he throws it away in a true, unfeigned fit of apathy.

The end of the novel can be read as either tragic or hopeful. Scarlett insists that she can get Rhett back and seems certain that she will go back to Tara, renew her strength, and continue fighting to survive and find happiness. The final phrase of the novel, "tomorrow is another day," could signify that the story does not end with the novel and that Scarlett will never give up in her quest for happiness. However, the same events can be read more darkly. Scarlett has lost Rhett's love, and although we have seen her survive through many hardships, she has never lost a husband she loved (she does not love either of her previous husbands). Her determination to return to Tara seems either valiant or deluded, for it is not entirely certain she will find happiness alone at Tara. Her final repetition of the mantra "tomorrow is another day" seems slightly disappointing. Scarlett always thinks she will put off moral considerations until an easier time, but as the novel ends she still has not reflected on her actions or learned from her wrongdoing. In some ways, she has not progressed at all.

Still, Scarlet does stand for the South and the South's resilience. When Scarlett chooses Rhett over Ashley it suggests that the life of the Old South, symbolized by Ashley, no longer exists. Like the Old South, Scarlett gives up hopeless dreams of a past life and looks to build a better future. Rhett scoffs at the South early on, but in the end he speaks sentimentally of his Southern heritage, so that when Scarlett chooses Rhett to love, she chooses the strange mixture of old and new that Rhett embodies. Like Scarlett, the South survives by changing with the changing times.

IMPORTANT QUOTATIONS EXPLAINED

1. Land is the only thing in the world that amounts to
    anything, for 'tis the only thing in this world that lasts.

Gerald O'Hara expresses this philosophy to Scarlett in Chapter II in
an effort to comfort her in her disappointment about Ashley
Wilkes's engagement to Melanie Hamilton. Gerald emphasizes the
importance of land, and of Tara in particular, foreshadowing the
end of the novel. Scarlett initially rejects the idea that land can be
more important than getting Ashley, the man she loves. However,
love of Tara increasingly motivates Scarlett's actions. Years later,
Ashley hands Scarlett a clump of Tara's dirt and tells her that she
loves Tara more than she loves him. Scarlett realizes that Ashley is
right. By the end of the novel, Scarlett has been abandoned by her
true love, and only the thought of Tara gives her hope and comfort.
Gerald's speech precisely predicts the end of the novel: Scarlett loses
her love for Ashley, her relationship with Melanie, and her marriage
with Rhett, and only Tara "lasts."

2. The people who have brains and courage come
through and the ones who haven't are winnowed out.

Ashley speaks these words to Scarlett in Chapter XXXI after the
Civil War has ended and he is living and working at Tara. Ashley
understands the divide between Old South and New South. As an
embodiment of the Old South, he finds himself completely out of
place after the war, his old way of life having disappeared. He excels
at a variety of leisurely skills practiced by Southern gentlemen:
riding horses, talking politics, and treating his peers with respect.
These skills are useless, however, in the harsh new world of Reconstruction, and Ashley cannot develop useful new skills. He struggles
and fails to labor on Tara and run Scarlett's sawmill for profit. Even
though Ashley cannot change while Scarlett excels at improvisation,
Ashley understands the absolute need for change while Scarlett does
not. Scarlett's survival instinct, not her analytical skills, guides her
behavior. Here Ashley provides commentary and analysis of the
South and of Scarlett's actions because Scarlett herself cannot. In
this quotation he expresses the idea that people like Scarlett have the
"brains and courage" to survive.

3. A startling thought this, that a woman could handle business matters as well as or better than a man, a revolutionary thought to Scarlett who had been reared in the tradition that men were omniscient and women none too bright.

This passage describes Scarlett's revelation after looking through Frank's poorly kept business ledgers, in Chapter XXXVI, that she could manage the mill more effectively than Frank. Though Scarlett is a strong, independent woman throughout the novel, this passage is the only statement that explicitly expresses ideas of gender equality. Many critics consider *Gone with the Wind* an early feminist work, a novel with a strong, smart, and capable female protagonist. Scarlett's budding feminist mentality prompts the shock and condemnation of her society, which frowns on the idea of a woman owning and running a mill. Scarlett has difficulty hiring a man from her class to run her mill because they are all ashamed to work for a woman. She finds support from Rhett alone, because like her he is ahead of his time. Though Rhett often treats Scarlett like a child or a pet, he is one of the few men who expects women to have a brain. He nurtures Scarlett's skills and encourages her to take advantage of her strengths.

4.   My dear, I don't give a damn.

Rhett utters this line, likely the most famous in the whole novel, in the final chapter, after Scarlett asks what she will do if Rhett abandons her. Rhett leaves Scarlett for the last time with these words, illustrating the love-hate nature of their relationship. The indifference and profanity in the line perfectly encapsulate Rhett's charming but spiteful character. Because Rhett hides his emotions, most notably his love for Scarlett, beneath a surface of nonchalance for so long, we cannot be sure of his exact feelings at this moment. The placement and alliteration of the words "dear" and "damn" seems to give them equal weight, accentuating the tension between the two. This line thus establishes a new conflict for Scarlett to resolve, which in turn gives us the sense that the story of Rhett and Scarlett does not end with Rhett's departure.

Incidentally, when the movie version of the novel was released in 1939, the use of the word "damn" set off a wave of publicity and scandal, and the director was fined $5,000 for its inclusion. Though "damn" appears frequently in the novel, such language was seen as explicitly objectionable in film, and its use cemented the line and the movie in popular culture history.

5.   I'll think of it all tomorrow, at Tara. I can stand it
      then. Tomorrow, I'll think of some way to get him
      back. After all, tomorrow is another day.

These words, Scarlett's personal motto, conclude *Gone with the
Wind*. Scarlett repeats some variation of this line several times over
the course of the novel when hardships plague her. She knows that
she often acts immorally and that she faces absurdly difficult cir-
cumstances, and to avoid feelings of guilt and helplessness she simply avoids reflecting on her life. Scarlett knows that eventually she
should mull over her plight, but she always puts it off until
another, different day, which never truly comes. But this refusal to
reflect is crucial to Scarlett's survival. Her attitude contrasts
directly with Ashley's obsession with the past and his inability to
let go of nostalgia and adapt to new times. Scarlett's determination
to believe that "tomorrow is another day" indicates her fundamental optimism about the future. Because Scarlett represents the
South, her optimism indicates Mitchell's general optimism about
the South's ability to survive in the face of change.

QUOTATIONS

KEY FACTS

FULL TITLE
Gone with the Wind

AUTHOR
Margaret Mitchell

TYPE OF WORK
Novel

GENRE
Romance novel; historical fiction; bildungsroman (novel that charts the maturation of the main character)

LANGUAGE
English

TIME AND PLACE WRITTEN
1926–1936; Atlanta

DATE OF FIRST PUBLICATION
1936

PUBLISHER
Houghton Mifflin

NARRATOR
The anonymous narrator speaks in the third person and is omniscient, having access to the thoughts, emotions, and histories of all characters and possessing insight into the context and consequences of events in the novel that the characters lack. The narrator generally voices the upper-class Southern perspective on the Civil War and slavery.

POINT OF VIEW
The narrator follows Scarlett almost exclusively, occasionally pulling back to give broad historical descriptions and analysis

TONE
The narrator treats the characters and the plot seriously but often criticizes characters who take themselves too seriously

TENSE
Past

SETTING (TIME)
1861–early 1870s

SETTING (PLACE)
Atlanta; Tara, the O'Hara plantation in northern Georgia

PROTAGONIST
Scarlett O'Hara

MAJOR CONFLICT
Scarlett struggles to find love, trying out Ashley Wilkes and Rhett Butler, while simultaneously trying to adjust to the changing face of the South

RISING ACTION
Scarlett confesses her love to Ashley; Scarlett marries Rhett; Scarlett and Ashley embrace

CLIMAX
Bonnie dies while horseback riding, breaking the tie that binds Rhett and Scarlett

FALLING ACTION
Scarlett falls down the stairs and miscarries; Rhett tells Melanie of his love for Scarlett; Melanie dies; Scarlett realizes that she loves Rhett, not Ashley; Rhett abandons Scarlett

THEMES
The transformation of Southern culture; overcoming adversity with willpower; the importance of land

MOTIFS
Female intelligence and capability; alcohol abuse; prostitution

SYMBOLS
Rhett Butler; Atlanta

FORESHADOWING
Gerald O'Hara's dangerous horse-jumping in Chapter II is part of a pattern of reckless behavior and hints at his later death, and that of Scarlett's daughte Bonnie Blue, both in riding accidents

KEY FACTS

Study Questions & Essay Topics

Study Questions

1. *In what way does Scarlett represent the Old South and in what way does she represent the New South? How does her transformation reflect the changes the South undergoes during and after the Civil War?*

From the beginning of the novel, Scarlett is a mixture of old and new. Her mother, Ellen, comes from an established aristocratic family and her father, Gerald, is a self-made immigrant. Scarlett admires her mother's refined manners and quiet strength, and she longs to please her, but this desire frequently conflicts with the strong, independent spirit Scarlett has inherited from Gerald. As Scarlett grows and society around her changes, she becomes less refined and more strong-willed.

Before the war, Scarlett obeys nearly all the rules of high-class Southern society, even the ones she finds unnatural. When the war begins, though, Scarlett finds that the social code relaxes, and she begins to indulge her natural instinct to break rules. Additionally, rule-breakers like Rhett become crucial to the South's survival. Scarlett becomes increasingly heedless of social mores after she returns to manage Tara and the South loses ground in the war. She becomes self-reliant and business-savvy, traits that would be shocking in an Old South woman but that ensure Scarlett's survival in the New South. During Reconstruction, Scarlett buys a sawmill and socializes with the Northerners in power, thumbing her nose at the rules of the Old South. Scarlett's journey from prewar belle to scrappy survivor to hardened opportunist parallels the journey of Southern culture before, during, and after the Civil War. After the corrupt period of Reconstruction, Scarlett goes back to Tara to regain her heritage, reclaiming her Old Southern roots but tempering them with new experience. So too does her Southern culture regain control of its political structures and rebuild a society that mixes the old world with the new one.

2. *Compare and contrast Ashley and Rhett. What cultural attitudes or ways of life do they embody?*

In some ways, Ashley and Rhett are opposites. Ashley is a blond, gentle dreamer; Rhett is a dark, mocking opportunist. Ashley becomes a Confederate hero in the Civil War; Rhett scorns the war until it is almost over and profits from scarcity in the South. The Southern aristocracy thinks highly of Ashley; everyone—including his own aristocratic family—looks down upon Rhett. Despite their differences, both Ashley and Rhett understand the change occurring in the South and the death of the Old South as they know it. Although Ashley willingly fights in the war and Rhett does not, they both think of the war in precisely the same way. Ashley writes to Melanie that he feels doubts about the Southern cause and the possibility of victory, and Rhett expresses similar views to horrified Southern men before the war begins. Ashley avoids reality, fighting for a cause he knows is lost and then letting Melanie and Scarlett take care of him, while Rhett follows the dictates of his common sense and relies only on himself. Ashley symbolizes the Old South that becomes obsolete after the war, and Rhett symbolizes the New South that rises up from Old Southern roots and adapts to postwar society.

Ashley and Rhett both love Scarlett and lust after her, but both push her away. Ashley chooses Melanie, the better social match, over Scarlett, the woman that fascinates him. Rhett mercilessly teases Scarlett and feigns indifference to her, terrified to reveal his feelings and invite the brutality with which she treats the men who love her. Both Ashley and Rhett are particularly fond of Melanie, who does not obsess them as Scarlett does but who comforts them with her traditional values and her nurturing.

3. *How are slavery and black people depicted in Gone with the Wind? Can the novel be labeled racist?*

In *Gone with the Wind,* Mitchell writes about slavery from the per-spective of Southern plantation owners. She depicts house slaves like Mammy and Pork as devoted and loving servants whom the whites treat like family. In the novel, all masters treat all slaves well. Although some admirable characters dislike slavery, Ashley and Frank among them, once the slaves are freed both the characters and the narrator describe blacks as "trashy," "insolent," and "creatures of small intelligence." Slaves and free blacks are often described as animals and compared to monkeys and dogs. All ex-Confederates in Scarlett's circle belong to the Ku Klux Klan, and both Tony Fon-taine and Rhett kill a black man with no feelings of remorse or guilt.

Mitchell paints a historically accurate picture of the brutal treat-ment of freed slaves, but she provides an extremely unrealistic pic-ture of the way slaves were treated before emancipation. While some white owners treated their slaves well, the rampant abuse of slaves in the South is will documented. The characters' contempt for freed slaves can be interpreted as a realistic depiction of Civil War–era rac-ism, but the narrator's racist attitude toward black people cannot be excused so easily. By current standards, the novel is shockingly rac-ist. By the standards of Mitchell's time, the novel's portrait of race relations is typical. Mitchell published her novel in the 1930s, when white acceptance of overt racism was not uncommon.

SUGGESTED ESSAY TOPICS

1. Is Scarlett O'Hara a feminist character? Explain why or why not, considering historical context, Scarlett's character traits, and her relationship with Rhett.

2. What values and lifestyles do Tara and Atlanta represent? How does Scarlett change as a result of her interactions with these two settings?

3. Discuss some of Scarlett's unscrupulous actions—for instance, her employment of convicts in the mill. How does she justify these actions? How do other characters react to her? Does the narrator judge her, defend her, or remain objective?

4. Discuss class issues in *Gone with the Wind*. How does Mitchell portray characters who do not belong to the white plantation-owning class? How do the Civil War and Reconstruction change class boundaries?

5. How do Gerald and Ellen influence Scarlett's character? What traits does she inherit from each?

6. What role does Melanie play in the novel? How and why does her relationship with Scarlett change over time?

REVIEW & RESOURCES

QUIZ

1. How many children does Scarlett have?

   A. One
   B. Two
   C. Three
   D. Four

2. Why does Archie oppose Scarlett's plan to lease convicts?

   A. It will lose money
   B. Convicts will threaten Scarlett's life
   C. He despises the ill treatment that leased convicts get
   D. It will threaten Archie's job

3. Why does Scarlett stay with Melanie when Atlanta is under attack?

   A. Scarlett loves Melanie
   B. Scarlett has made a promise to Ashley
   C. Scarlett loves Atlanta
   D. Scarlett is afraid to leave

4. Who saves Scarlett from the attack in Shantytown?

   A. Uncle Peter
   B. Rhett
   C. Ashley
   D. Big Sam

5. How does Gerald die?

   A. Trying to jump a fence on a horse
   B. Fighting at Gettysburg
   C. Alcohol poisoning
   D. Typhoid fever

6. How old is Scarlett at the beginning of the novel?

    A. Twenty-four
    B. Twenty-one
    C. Sixteen
    D. Nine

7. Who is Scarlett's second husband?

    A. Charles
    B. Frank
    C. Rhett
    D. Ashley

8. What phrase does Scarlett repeat to herself in difficult times?

    A. "I'll do it for Ashley"
    B. "The South is *gone with the wind*, but I am still here"
    C. "I'll always have Tara"
    D. "I'll think about it tomorrow"

9. Who delivers Melanie's child?

    A. Scarlett
    B. Prissy
    C. Dilcey
    D. Mammy

10. How does Rhett make money during the war?

    A. Blackmailing
    B. Selling war bonds
    C. Running blockades
    D. Organizing fundraisers

11. Who tries to buy Tara from Scarlett?

    A. Will Benteen
    B. Jonas Wilkerson
    C. Rhett
    D. Johnnie Gallegher

12. Who catches Scarlett and Ashley embracing?

    A.   Rhett
    B.   Melanie
    C.   Mrs. Elsing and Mrs. Merriwether
    D.   India Wilkes and Archie

13. What, according to Ashley, does Scarlett love more
    than she loves him?

    A.   Tara
    B.   Rhett
    C.   The South
    D.   Alcohol

14. Where does Scarlett plan to go at the end of the novel?

    A.   Charleston
    B.   Aunt Pittypat's house
    C.   Tara
    D.   Boston

15. Who testifies on behalf of the Klansmen after
    Frank is killed?

    A.   Scarlett
    B.   Belle Watling
    C.   Aunt Pittypat
    D.   Wade

16. How does Bonnie die?

    A.   Typhoid fever
    B.   Falling down the stairs
    C.   Drowning
    D.   Jumping her horse over an obstacle

17. Why does Ashley refuse to marry Scarlett?

    A.   Scarlett is not wealthy enough
    B.   They are too different
    C.   He secretly loves her mother
    D.   He does not love Scarlett

REVIEW & RESOURCES

18. Why does Scarlett slap Prissy?

    A.   Prissy slapped Scarlett first

    B.   Prissy tried to escape slavery

    C.   Prissy lied about her midwifery experience

    D.   Prissy taunted Scarlett

19. Who gives Bonnie her nickname?

    A.   Melanie

    B.   Ashley

    C.   Uncle Peter

    D.   Aunt Pittypat

20. According to Old Miss Fontaine, what is the secret to life?

    A.   Being kind even in times of trouble

    B.   Maintaining old values and lifestyles

    C.   Following one's heart

    D.   Changing with the changing times

21. Why does Rhett abandon Scarlett and Melanie outside Atlanta?

    A.   He is afraid of the dark

    B.   He is bitter that Scarlett rejected him

    C.   He is joining the Confederate army

    D.   He thinks his presence would endanger them

22. Why is Rhett put in jail?

    A.   He killed a Yankee

    B.   He killed a black man

    C.   He is implicated in a Ku Klux Klan raid

    D.   He raped Scarlett

23. Where does Rhett usually spend time after he fights with Scarlett?

    A.   Charleston

    B.   Melanie's house

    C.   The fish pond

    D.   Belle Watling's place

24. Why does Scarlett have a miscarriage?

    A. She falls down the stairs after trying to strike Rhett
    B. She induces it on purpose
    C. Rhett hits her in the stomach
    D. She drinks too much

25. What is the final line of the novel?

    A. "Alas, the Old South is gone with the wind"
    B. "The sun will come out tomorrow"
    C. "My dear, I don't give a damn"
    D. "After all, tomorrow is another day"

SUGGESTIONS FOR FURTHER READING

BEYE, CHARLES ROWAN. "Gone with the Wind, and Good Riddance." Southwest Review 78.3 (1993): 366–380.

HARWELL, RICHARD, ED. *Gone with the Wind as Book and Film.* Columbia: University of South Carolina Press, 1983.

HAWKINS, HARRIETT. *Classics and Trash: Traditions and Taboos in High Literature and Popular Modern Genres.* London: Harvester Wheatsheaf, 1990.

LEFF, LEONARD J. "David Selznick's Gone with the Wind: 'The Negro Problem.'" The Georgia Review 38.1 (Spring 1984): 146–164.

PYRON, DARDEN ASBURY. *Recasting: Gone with the Wind in American Culture.* Miami: University Presses of Florida, 1983.

RANDALL, ALICE. *The Wind Done Gone: A Novel.* Boston: Houghton Mifflin Company, 2001.

TAYLOR, HELEN. *Scarlett's Women: Gone with the Wind and Its Female Fans.* New Brunswick, New Jersey: Rutgers University Press, 1989.

SPARKNOTES
TEST PREPARATION
GUIDES

The SparkNotes team figured it was time to cut standardized tests down to size. We've studied the tests for you, so that SparkNotes test prep guides are:

Smarter:
Packed with critical-thinking skills and test-
taking strategies that will improve your score.

Better:
Fully up to date, covering all new features of the tests,
with study tips on every type of question.

Faster:
Our books cover exactly what you need to
know for the test. No more, no less.

SparkNotes Guide to the SAT & PSAT
SparkNotes Guide to the SAT & PSAT—Deluxe Internet Edition
SparkNotes Guide to the ACT
SparkNotes Guide to the ACT—Deluxe Internet Edition
SparkNotes Guide to the SAT II Writing
SparkNotes Guide to the SAT II U.S. History
SparkNotes Guide to the SAT II Math Ic
SparkNotes Guide to the SAT II Math IIc
SparkNotes Guide to the SAT II Biology
SparkNotes Guide to the SAT II Physics

SPARKNOTES STUDY GUIDES: